Investment Banking

Investment Banking

Addressing the Management Issues

Steven I. Davis

First published 2003 by
PALGRAVE MACMILLAN
Houndmills, Basingstoke, Hampshire RG21 6XS and
175 Fifth Avenue, New York, N.Y. 10010
Companies and representatives throughout the world

PALGRAVE MACMILLAN is the global academic imprint of the Palgrave
Macmillan division of St. Martin's Press, LLC and of Palgrave Macmillan Ltd.
Macmillan® is a registered trademark in the United States, United Kingdom
and other countries. Palgrave is a registered trademark in the European
Union and other countries.

ISBN 1–4039–0144–9

This book is printed on paper suitable for recycling and made from fully
managed and sustained forest sources.

A catalogue record for this book is available from the British Library.

Library of Congress Cataloging-in-Publication Data
Davis, Steven I.
    Investment banking : addressing the management issues / Steven I. Davis.
        p.   cm.
    Includes bibliographical references and index.
    ISBN 1–4039–0144–9
    1. Investment banking.   2. Investment banking—Case studies.   I. Title.
    HG4534 .D38 2002
    332.66′068—dc21
                                                                    2002030805

10   9   8   7   6   5   4   3   2   1
12   11   10   09   08   07   06   05   04   03

Printed and bound in Great Britain by
Antony Rowe Ltd, Chippenham and Eastbourne

Contents

List of Figures

List of Tables

1
Introduction

The world of investment banking has long exerted a fascination for academics, management consultants, and financial analysts as well as practitioners. Today the fascination has reached fever pitch as the business, having grown globally at a phenomenal rate in the 1990s of perhaps three times GDP in key markets like the US and Europe, faces some of the consequences of its turbulent existence. From essentially a cottage industry a few decades ago, it has attracted investors with returns on capital rarely seen in other financial businesses, the cream of the world's business schools with compensation levels inconceivable in earlier eras, and competitors from the world's wholesale banks desperate to preserve at least a portion of their corporate banking franchise.

For me, the fascination of the business lies in the management issues raised in this headlong but volatile expansion. A flurry of recent consultant and analyst reports focuses on the outlook for the sector and its likely winners and losers. A handful of books have been written by journalists and other outsiders on some of the more dramatic case studies such as the collapse of Barings, Lehman Brothers' turmoil in the 1980s, and the host of British merchant banks who succumbed to the onslaught of US investment banks following Big Bang in 1986.[1] Only a very few actual practitioners have described how their institution rose or fell over the past two decades.[2]

But today's generic management issues remain largely unexplored. For example:

- how can management cope with the high and rising cost base in a sector distinguished by revenues which seem to collapse with some regularity every three or four years?

- can they reconcile the demands of the industry's outside stockholders with those of key professionals well known for their ability to 'walk' if their perceived financial needs are not met?
- can today's massive and complex global competitors achieve the flexibility, innovation and level of client service which have long distinguished the sector's leaders?
- is management capable of dealing not only with its traditional market risk exposure but also credit and operational risk?
- is there a viable role for the mid-sized banks in markets like Europe who are now being squeezed between the global and smaller specialist firms?

The answers to these and other questions should enable us to address those of universal interest to all constituencies: *how might the business evolve in the future, and who are the likely winners and losers?*

The management issues of an earlier era were explored in a seminal book written in 1988 by Professor Dwight Crane and his colleagues at the Harvard Business School. *Doing Deals* ably articulated the unique structures and processes of the business which still distinguish it from all other financial services.[3] Yet investment banking has moved on to levels of size and complexity difficult to contemplate in 1986. Leadership in investment banking is now being sought by the world's largest financial institutions rather than the few hundred specialists in First Boston Corporation in New York described by *Doing Deals* in 1986. The well-known forces of globalization, deregulation, securitization and rise in investor wealth have enabled these securities firms to marginalize many traditional corporate or wholesale banks.

So it's time to revisit the issues!

My methodology once again is to rely heavily on the frank insights of senior practitioners across the business, supplemented by the observations of expert witnesses such as management consultants and industry analysts as well as the elaborate database now available. In early 2002 I interviewed 40 such individuals in more than 25 investment banks, from chief executives to function heads, including all of the eight global firms, most of the mid-sized European banks with investment banking aspirations, plus a number of advisory or sectoral specialists. In addition, I met with 15 independent experts: management consultants, buy and sell-side analysts, academics and rating agencies.

My approach was quite simple: to determine what issues my inter-viewees felt to be central to their success, what is best practice in addressing those issues, and what actual outcome do they anticipate? The list of firms interviewed is provided in Appendix 1 at the end of the book. Where appropriate, and with their concurrence, I have given the name of my interviewee in the numerous direct quotations which I consider essential for an understanding of the real world in which these professionals operate. My own conclusions have been limited essentially to the final chapter.

In the fast-moving world of investment banking, definitions are necessary but often inadequate. In this book we define investment banking essentially as the intermediation between issuers and investors through the core functions of advisory/M & A, debt capital markets and equity capital markets. While related businesses such as asset management, private equity and private banking may be important to individual institutions, they merit a volume of their own! Lending is incorporated in debt capital markets as a sub-set, albeit an increasingly important one, of the debt product. The so-called 'global bulge group', now widely assumed to constitute the eight firms which appear in Table 2.3 and Figure 3.3, refers to the firms with global reach which now dominate the league tables in key businesses. Within this category are the so-called 'pure' investment banks, essentially the three US leaders – Goldman Sachs, Merrill Lynch and Morgan Stanley Dean Witter. I had great difficulty labelling another segment which I have termed 'mid-sized bank' – essentially European universal banks below the global players. Chapter 11 provides a number of alternative labels used by others. Other definitions are incorporated in the text to follow.

I have tried to analyse the sector as a global business, with interviewees and data from the three core regions of the US (Americas), Europe and Japan (Asia). Readers will detect a modest bias in favour of Europe in view of the increased focus by the US leaders on that relatively undeveloped market as well as the current key issue of the fate of the numerous Europe-based universal banks struggling to define a viable strategy.

My grateful thanks go first to the senior professionals who gave generously of their time for the interview as well as their frank insights on the issues of the day. To me, these insights represent the unique value of this book, and I only hope I have done justice to their views and experience. Special thanks also go to the multitude of firms and individuals who made available the fruits of their own research and data collection: Jim Freeman of Freeman & Company; Brad Hintz of Sanford Bernstein; senior consultants at McKinsey & Co., Greenwich Associates, Boston Consulting Group, and Oliver, Wyman & Co.; as well as bank analysts at Lehman Brothers, Salomon Smith Barney, and UBS Warburg. And to

Hannah Seeds, who patiently, creatively, and ably translated my draft into a fully-fledged book, I am particularly indebted!

I must also acknowledge a personal agenda in writing this book. My initial career decision, to join JP Morgan on Wall Street fresh out of business school, was a deliberate choice of commercial banking rather than investment banking. My instincts then were that the world of investment banking was beyond my own limited capabilities, but I revisited the issue when I set up an American-owned merchant bank in London – a half-way house at the time between commercial and investment banking. As a bank strategy consultant since then, a good portion of my work has involved tracking the demise of traditional corporate, or wholesale, banking and the corresponding rise of the investment banker. With this book I can at least satisfy some of my lifetime fascination with the career path not chosen!

The book begins with Chapter 2, a brief historical record of how we got here from there. It tracks the rise and rise of the US investment banks which now dominate the commanding heights of global investment banking, as well as the efforts of European and other banks to challenge this hegemony. An extended Chapter 3 analyses today's dominant business models. Sections of this chapter examine in some detail the key dimensions of product, geography and client segment which constitute a business strategy.

In Chapter 4 I explore the fascinating human dimension of investment banking: the unique culture of its practitioners and their leadership, which drive several of the following chapters on structure, process and compensation. Chapter 5 addresses the equally unique structure and other management processes of this highly creative, volatile and horizontally-configured business. This is followed by Chapter 6 on the central issue of compensation in the battle to attract, motivate and retain the key professionals who are the heart of the business.

In Chapter 7 I address the issue of cost management: how does management adjust a high and growing cost base to a highly volatile revenue stream without destroying its ability to meet customer needs? Investment banking is all about managing risk, and Chapter 8 examines the risk issues which are central to the thoughts of today's management teams. Chapter 9 analyses the lessons from expansion by merger and acquisition – a key issue today as a growing number of competitors resort to such strategies to compete with the leaders which have essentially grown organically.

In our interviews I took straw poll to identify competitors which were viewed as the best positioned or most feared competitor as well as those with uniquely successful operating models. In Chapter 10 we profile the three winners from this rough-and-ready sample, as well as giving brief descriptions of four other successful mid-sized or specialist firms whose record confirms that the investment banking world is not entirely composed of giant global entities!

With the investment banking business passing through one of the longest revenue droughts in its volatile history, predicting the future is on the minds of all of the interviewees. Chapter 11 summarizes their views on how the business might evolve in the medium or longer term. Finally, in Chapter 12 we offer our own comments on these views as well as our own conclusions for the future.

To repeat a point made earlier, my focus throughout the book is on management issues: what are they, who is relatively successful in addressing them, and how might these efforts bear fruit in the future? I hope that the reader finds of interest at least some of the insights in the following pages!

2
A Brief History Lesson: Getting Here From There

"A veritable tsunami has torn through the markets."
– Greenwich Associates

A number of environmental trends as well as the creativity and dynamism of their professional teams have shaped today's investment banks. Casting an eye back to, say, the beginning of post-Second World War deregulation in the mid-1970s provides an essential understanding of today's issues.

Let's examine first the external trends. Most analysts agree that the key drivers of the phenomenal secular growth of the business have been GDP growth and stock market prices. Research confirms the intuitive conclusion that volumes and profits in the key products of M & A advisory and primary equity issues essentially track equity prices.[4] Thus the unprecedented global stock market boom which ended in early 2000 sustained an equally remarkable decade of double-digit annual earnings growth for investment bankers. Related products such as equity derivatives and secondary trading in turn track equity issuance, while debt issuance tends to follow interest rate movements.

Table 2.1 from a recent study by Moody's provides an excellent summary of the relative impact of some key drivers of the sector's growth.

Thus over the 1983–2000 span, while global GDP grew at a 6 per cent compound annual rate, global debt issuance expanded by 18 per cent and global equity by 12 per cent per annum. In tandem, worldwide equity market capitalization soared at a rate of 14 per cent per annum.

A second driver in recent decades has been globalization. This over-used term can mean different things to different constituencies, but to investment bankers it means essentially cross-border investment flows.

Table 2.1 Relative growth in key drivers of investment banking expansion, 1983–2000 ($ in billion; years ending 31/12)

	1983	1988	1993	2000	CAGR 83–00 (%)
Worldwide GDP ($ trillion)	12	19	24	31	6
Worldwide mergers & acquisitions ($)	96	527	460	3 461	23
Worldwide equity issued ($)	50	51	172	322	12
Worldwide debt issues ($)	146	631	1 546	2 604	18
Worldwide equity market capitalization ($)	3 384	9 728	14 016	32 260	14
NYSE average daily volume (shares, millions)	85	162	265	1 042	16
Worldwide pension assets ($)	1 900	3 752	6 560	9 100	10
US mutual funds assets ($)	293	810	2 075	6 965	20

Sources: Moody's, Thomson Financial Securities Data, Strategic Insight, SIA, World Bank.

Cross-border mergers and acquisitions in the developed world as well as direct and portfolio investment in emerging markets have fuelled the profitability of the handful of banks, primarily US-based, who have had the relationships and networks to capture these flows. As indicated by Table 2.1, global M & A surged over the period by a remarkable 23 per cent per annum.

The accumulation of assets managed by institutions has been a third key factor in the evolution of investment banks. GNP growth has generated personal wealth, but it has been the growing share of that wealth managed by institutions such as pension funds which has created a vibrant market for investment banks in their role as intermediaries between issuers and investors. As the US has led this institutional development, once again it is the US investment banks who have occupied a privileged competitive position. Table 2.1 thus indicates a 10 per cent annual expansion of worldwide pension assets as well as a remarkable 20 per cent annual growth of US mutual fund assets.

Securitization – the shift of assets from commercial bank balance sheets to investors via the capital markets – has been a particular boon to investment banks. Fuelled by such drivers as investor demand for rated paper, the need of many banks to release regulatory capital, and the investment bankers' creativity in creating yet new securitization concepts, securitization has represented a direct transfer in economic clout from commercial to investment banks.

Figure 2.1   Disaggregation in Europe tracks US Model

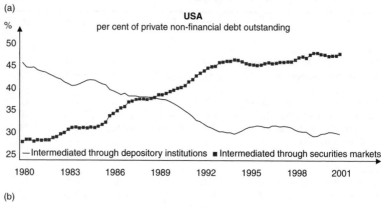

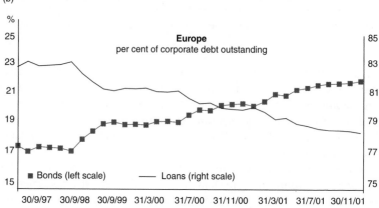

Source: (a) Federal Reserve Board, Morgan Stanley. (b) ECB.

Figure 2.1 tracks this shift in the form of the percentage of assets held in the US and Europe held by commercial banks as opposed to investors. The steady decline in the proportion of bank lending from about 46 per cent of the total to 30 per cent in the US over the period 1980–2001 has been matched several years later in Europe. As we discuss below, securitization is only one of the products successfully exported to Europe by US investment banks in their invasion during the 1990s.

A final driver has been deregulation. Seminal events, such as the 1975 deregulation of US brokerage commissions and the 1986 Big Bang in the UK permitting banks to own brokers, have triggered consolidation on a massive scale not only within the sector but also the eventual fusion of commercial and investment banking. Price deregulation in the

US in 1975 drove a collapse in brokerage revenues which forced brokers to sell out or develop a better business model. Breaking down the barriers between brokers and banks in the UK led to the almost total absorption of the brokerage community into larger, more diversified entities. Over this period, the distinction in the US between brokers – essentially trading in the secondary markets on behalf of clients – and investment banks, which provide corporate advice and manage primary issuance, has disappeared. What we term 'investment banks' in this book are essentially the survivors in the US who have given their label to the global sector.

Yet these external developments only set the stage for a transformation of the business. Innovation, aggressive expansion and the overriding drive for earnings and market share on the part of highly-motivated investment bankers have produced the increasingly polarized business analysed in the balance of this book.

In the US in particular, these bankers quickly learned some basic lessons. First, market share dominance generally leads to superior profits – the so-called operational leverage which is part of the sector's vocabulary – as revenues tend to be concentrated disproportionately among the handful of leaders in a given segment. Secondly, the universal phenomenon of exponentially-growing profitability from selling incremental products to the same client is reinforced in investment banking by the logical linkages between products. Thus M & A advisory may lead to mandates for other transactions – a relationship which we discuss in the following chapter. Finally, innovation can be exported to other markets such as Japan and Europe, less-developed financial communities which may therefore offer superior growth potential.

It is this comprehensive invasion of the major markets of Europe and Japan which has shaped today's investment banking marketplace.

In Continental Europe, the so-called 'universal' bank has dominated the scene since the late nineteenth century when most of these institutions were created. Their universality extended to investment banking in the sense that a vast retail customer base was a natural market for the securities issued in the local currency by the bank's primary markets arm. The relative absence of large institutional investors characteristic of the US and UK was thus not an issue: the primary market power of the bank was sustained by internal placing power. Each national market had its own unique structure and technology. Thus *banques d'affaires* in France carried out most functions now associated with investment banking, while in Germany *Universalbanken* played a similar role as well being as a major supplier of credit.

Europe's largest national investment banking market, the UK, had its own unique structure inherited from centuries of historical evolution as a global financial centre. Securities distribution was the domain of stock-brokers, secondary market trading that of the jobbers, and advisory services largely the province of the merchant banks. Big Bang threw them all together, and the US investment banks with their integrated model were the principal beneficiaries of the stresses and dislocation which followed Big Bang.

In Japan, which inherited the US Glass-Steagall-type legal barriers between investment and commercial banking, retail placing power also underpinned the primary market capability of the large brokers like Nomura who dominated the market. As in the US, the commercial banks with their vast balance sheets and retail client bases were legally excluded from playing any significant role in the underwriting and distribution of securities until the late 1990s.

By the late 1980s and early 1990s, the rapidly-integrating US investment banking community had developed the global business model we describe in more detail in Chapter 3. Its key elements are a full product array across the range of advisory, debt and equity products; global distribution through units based in the key national markets; global research organized on a sectoral basis and often covering several thousand leading companies; and client coverage of the world's largest generators of fee income among issuers and institutional investors.

Led by the trio of Goldman Sachs, Merrill Lynch and Morgan Stanley, US investment banks first assaulted London and Tokyo, before moving on to other large national markets. Their dominance of the US market, which generates well over half of the total global fee pool, generated the profits necessary to subsidize a massively expensive, long-term penetration of these markets. With their US clients representing one leg of most cross-border M & A transactions and their global research and origination capability, they understandably won market share in this growing and lucrative business. Exporting product innovation in highly profitable, booming sectors such as derivatives and securitization provided a useful entry strategy, while aggressive relationship building with local clients steadily displaced many incumbent competitors.

In Europe, the introduction of the euro in 1999 provided a major impetus to this invasion. The primary markets strategies of the local universal banks had been underpinned by their dominance of issuance of debt and equity in the local currency naturally preferred by their investment community. The loss of this competitive advantage with the introduction of the euro offered a golden opportunity for newcomers who were now able to compete on equal terms in the new European currency. Almost as important was the creation of a major new capital pool which approximated the US dollar market in size and enabled the US banks to argue that they were best equipped to help clients exploit such a market. Using the US as a model, they also argued that Europe was ripe for the type of sectoral consolidation experienced in their home market.

During the decade of the 1990s, the impact was dramatic in both Europe and Japan.

In Japan, to quote a publication by the leading research firm Greenwich Associates:

> *"A veritable tsunami has torn through the markets, wreaking havoc with the old industry structure and bringing global best practice to Japan. Today four of the five market leaders are Western firms, with talented Japanese people doing business the Western way."*[5]

The fifth of these leaders is Nomura Securities, which remains the dominant domestic investment bank on the strength of its vast retail network and placing power. In 1991, when a different tsunami – the so-called 'wall of money' represented by Japanese investment overseas – threatened to overwhelm western competitors, Nomura was the global leader in the investment banking league tables.

By 1993, however, Nomura did not even figure in the more relevant league tables based on actual fees paid by issuers for M & A as well as debt and equity issuance. Table 2.2 lists the global leaders on this basis since 1993.

Nomura and its Japanese peers were not able to replicate the US global model. A senior international investment banker at Nomura explains why:

> *"If your economy is growing, it's easier to succeed as a financial institution. In 1988, Nomura was on top of the world – it rode the Japanese success story. A strong domestic cash flow could have been used to subsidize growth in other markets. But the tables were turned, and Japan went into recession, while the US boomed. The US investment banks 'did' the Japanese*

Table 2.2 Global investment banking fees received: league tables by individual institution (%)

1993		1997		2001	
Merrill Lynch	8.4	Merrill Lynch	7.2	Merrill Lynch	9.0
Salomon Smith Barney	6.7	CSFB	6.9	Goldman Sachs	7.5
UBS Warburg	6.2	Goldman Sachs	6.7	CSFB	7.2
CSFB	6.2	Salomon Smith Barney	6.7	Salomon Smith Barney	6.7
Goldman Sachs	5.8	Morgan Stanley	6.5	Morgan Stanley	6.3
Morgan Stanley	5.8	JP Morgan	5.3	JP Morgan	5.5
Lehman	4.0	UBS Warburg	4.0	UBS Warburg	4.6
JP Morgan	2.9	Deutsche	3.6	Lehman	3.6
Deutsche	2.8	Lehman	2.9	Deutsche	3.5
Bear Stearns	1.7	Bear Stearns	2.1	Bank of America	2.4
Top 10 Total	50.5		51.9		56.3

Source: Freeman & Co.

thing by taking the long term view – 10 years – to build abroad. The Japanese banks never did. And the US and European investment banks are still building in Japan."

His experience is amplified by the Greenwich research analysis:

"The big stockbrokerage business in Japan was ... retail stockbrokerage ... The particular needs and interests of institutional investors-for thorough research, professional service, and for liquidity through block trading ... were largely unmet as the major stockbrokers concentrated on their retail business ... Outsiders brought a revolution to the stockbrokerage business."[6]

Martin O'Neil, a former JP Morgan banker in the Far East, confirms that:

"Japan was the first and mother of all emerging markets. Japan is just a trading floor for foreign banks who arbitrage the inefficiencies of an arcane third-world financial system."

In the UK, the foreign invasion was equally transforming. The literature of UK merchant banking post-Big Bang in 1986 is replete with failures of both commercial (or trading) banks and traditional merchant banks to meet the US global competition. The former balked at committing the resources and time needed to create a competitive institution, while the merchant banks suffered from integration problems, a limited capital base, and lack of experience in melding the advisory, trading and distribution functions. The ultimate defeat came with the sale of Britain's leading investment bank, SG Warburg, to Swiss Bank Corporation in 1995 following aborted merger negotiations, heavy investment in building a global capability, and losses following the 1994 fixed income collapse.

The sad tale of what has become known as the 'Wimbledon' phenomenon – hosting a major global event without providing any of the major competitors – is well recorded in the literature. From the commercial banking side, here are some observations from the efforts by National Westminster Bank and Barclays Bank to play a role on the investment banking stage.

Philip Augar, a senior executive at NatWest Markets, recounts his experience with a reluctant commercial bank senior management and board of directors:

> *"A lack of support for the investment banking initiative which ran through the NatWest group was kept alive and fostered into a rich seam by the poor results and bad publicity [from recent losses]. This occurred at the Board level where there were regular debates about the investment bank's future, through the all-powerful office of the group chief executive which initiated frequent formal and informal reviews of the strategy, through personnel at the bank's senior and middle level management."*[7]

Augar quotes Keith Brown, a senior banking executive who worked at first a UK and later a US investment bank:

> *"I realized what a lot of rank amateurs we and the rest of the UK houses were. Morgan Stanley had a tradition of investment banking, built up over a long period. Investment banking was a core and serious part of the business. They understood equity markets, how to operate in a free market and above all how to approach the corporate sector. They understood the value of financial discipline and how to reward and evaluate staff. They followed a pan-European approach and understood that events in one market can influence another."*[8]

A similar tale of woe emerged from Barclays Bank: lack of commitment from top management and the Board, lack of patience and recognition of the need to build a business over a period of years rather than months, and unwillingness to accept the risks inherent in the business.

In 1997 both banks exited the advisory and equity businesses.

A somewhat different story emerged from the British merchant banks, who, unlike the commercial banks, had no highly profitable retail business on which to fall back. The author of a book on the demise of Morgan Grenfell, ultimately sold in 1990 to Deutsche Bank, remarks:

> *"The bank was an operation riddled with cultural conflict between brokers, jobbers and bankers, bound together only by a common love of money and lacking in any distinctive esprit de corps. The hiring spree had only added an unsustainable cost base to the already formidable problems ... All merchant banks lacked management. It was no use adjuring young merchant bankers to 'Pick up the ball and run with it' in the securities markets where they had not yet learned even the rules of association football. As new markets erupted across the financial spectrum, banks impulsively pushed pawns into markets where kings were called for."[9]*

Yet the victory was not easily achieved. The history of Goldman Sachs, one of the first US banks to attack the key UK market, reveals both the extent of the preparatory work needed as well as the internal conflict generated in a partnership by the need to invest heavily for a long-term and uncertain pay-off outside the core US market. John Whitehead, the firm's co-CEO at the time and author of its global strategy, faced strong internal resistance to the costs and potential cultural conflict represented by expansion in London:

> *"It fell to me to spend some time thinking about the long term. I focused on two strategies: broadening the firm's product line and becoming a competitor outside the US. We simply had to build our capabilities in London and Tokyo ... I tend to deal with conflict by persuasion. We weren't a dictatorship, and I'd listen to all the objections and perhaps back away if others disagreed. There were a few occasions when persuasion didn't work and we simply had to decide, but it's so much better to get group acceptance. I'm an incrementalist, not a plunger!"[10]*

And Goldman had to work extremely hard to win the senior relationships in the UK on which its business model is based. An apocryphal story

Figure 2.2   US global bulge group wins market share in Europe

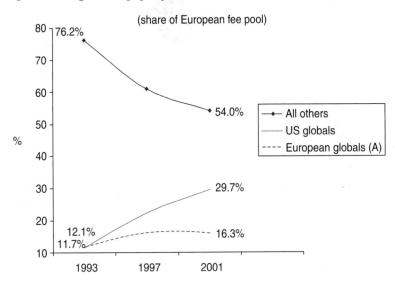

Note: (A) CSFB, UBS Warburg, Deutsche Bank.
Source: Freeman & Co.

quoted in the *Financial Times* describes the efforts of John Thornton, later Goldman's co-CEO:

> *"On at least one occasion Mr. Thornton turned up at the office of a chief executive at a leading British company without an appointment. He just sat and waited until he got one and was awarded the mandate he was after."*[11]

The trauma at the major Continental European universal banks was less dramatic but certainly transforming in its ultimate impact. Figure 2.2 plots the steady inroads made by the top 10 investment banks – essential the global elite – in the European fee pool between 1993 and 2001. Thus the balance remaining, largely for national competitors, has shrunk from 76.2 per cent to 54.0 per cent between 1993 and 2001.

A survey conducted by the author for Salomon Brothers at the end of 1993 – in the midst of this turmoil – of banks in nine countries outside the US revealed a remarkable number who aspired then to a global investment banking role. The study interviewed a total of 11 non-US banks (essentially from the UK, France, Germany and Switzerland) committed to a global investment banking strategy, with others reconciled to a regional or national role.

Among the study's conclusions which might be of interest in the light of subsequent events were the following:

- the global leadership of the US bulge group (essentially the three institutions listed on page 3) is not likely to be shaken;
- the only competitor likely to join the ranks of the US bulge group is JP Morgan;
- strength in one's home market outside the US is not a sufficient base for a global strategy;
- even the major Swiss and German universal banks do not have the culture, skills and global reach/distribution to compete successfully with the US leaders;
- niches (such as derivatives and emerging markets) can form the basis for a limited investment banking strategy. Special praise was awarded to Barings for its niche strategy in Asia;
- a functional rather than geographic structure is a critical success factor, with the commercial and investment banking functions effectively merged into one unit.

With 20/20 hindsight, one of the many weaknesses of this survey was ignoring the potential for the consolidation which has since transformed once again the investment banking landscape. Two of the three Swiss banks interviewed (Union Bank of Switzerland and Swiss Bank Corporation) merged to create a real global contender in UBS Warburg; Crédit Suisse bought Donaldson, Lufkin and Jenrette; JP Morgan did indeed make it into the global bulge group by merging with Chase; Deutsche Bank acquired Bankers Trust and transformed its strategy at the same time, and Citigroup created another powerhouse by linking its wholesale banking business with Schroders, Salomon Brothers and Smith Barney.

A footnote to this saga was the prescient executive from Chemical Bank, the predecessor to Chase, who told the interviewer in 1993 that Chemical planned to become a global player by the year 2000 – exactly the year JP Morgan was absorbed by Chase to create such a global leader! With regard to some of the other prophesies, we invite the reader to continue his journey!

Table 2.3 lists the mergers and acquisitions which have created new global contenders.

Less visible has been the retreat of many universal banks from their global or even regional aspirations. Niches such as emerging markets and derivatives have failed to prevent global players from entering and

Table 2.3 Breaking into the premier league – mergers & acquisitions by leading universal banks

Citigroup	CSFB	Deutsche	JP Morgan	UBS Warburg
Citibank	Crédit Suisse	Deutsche Bank	Manufacturers Hanover	Swiss Bank
Salomon Brothers	First Boston	Morgan Grenfell	Chemical	Phillips & Drew
Smith Barney	Donaldson, Lufkin & Jenrette	Alex Brown	Chase Manhattan	S.G. Warburg
Schroders	Pershing	Bankers Trust	Hambrecht & Quist	O'Connor
			Robert Fleming	Dillon Read
			Beacon Group	Paine Webber
			JP Morgan	

Source: Oliver, Wyman & Co.; Morgan Stanley Research.

eventually dominating these sectors. And niches can contribute to the downfall and disappearance of competitors – not only the ill-fated Drexel Burnham in junk bonds but also Barings' failure to supervise its niche business in Singapore.

The advance of the global leaders was not thrown off course by the periodic setbacks which have shaken investment banking roughly every three to four years. The global stock market collapse in 1987, severe operating losses in the US in 1990–91, the 1994 bond market shock, and the losses suffered in Russia and the hedge fund debacle in 1998: from each shock the global leaders have emerged with their collective dominance intact. And the current revenue drought initiated by the collapse of global stock markets in 2000 seems to bear out the lessons of the past.

The result of these tectonic shifts is a group of eight acknowledged global competitors, flanked by a larger number of mid-sized competitors aspiring generally to national or regional leadership, and a third group of advisory or sectoral specialists. In the chapters to follow we shall evaluate their business and operating models and offer some observations on their ultimate fate in Chapters 11 and 12.

3

The Business Model: Products, Clients and Markets

"Our engine is powerful; now we need a larger racetrack."
– Walter Gubert, JP Morgan

The starting point for our analysis is an investment bank's strategy: which clients or sectors are targeted, which products are offered, and in what geographical markets is the bank active. In today's jargon, it is the business model. This chapter will examine in turn each of these critical dimensions, with a particular focus on the three central product areas of advisory services, equity and debt.

3.1 Products

Arguably the defining characteristic of most investment banks is their range of products and services.

A number of forces drive them to achieve the broadest possible product array. First is the functional relationship among the various product categories. At the top of the decision-making pyramid for issuers is advisory, or M & A. Working closely with the client Chief Executive Officer (CEO), the banker provides advice which is not only a highly profitable business in itself but also leads to transactions he may manage – new debt and equity issues, leveraged buyouts, divestitures and structured finance. These transactions can generate additional investment banking revenues in the form of derivatives to hedge or leverage exposure, secondary trading and market making of the issues floated, or new products triggered by the issuance chain. An aggressive investment bank understandably wants to keep as many of these revenue-generating opportunities in-house as possible rather than lose them to rival firms. A senior London-based banker describes the challenge:

> "*Investment banking has lots of different pieces – five key businesses with gigantic synergy between them if they work in sync. When you're an investment banker, you have legally acceptable insider knowledge. At the top of the pyramid we're legitimately insiders – like a surgeon, you allow him to cut into you. We give value-added by sitting on that borderline. But the five key businesses have to work together to get full power.*"

Diversification is another driver for broadening the product array. While activity in most investment banking products, as indicated in Chapter 2, is tied to GDP and stock price development, others are linked to interest rate trends and other factors. In 2001–02, for example, booming fixed income revenues in a favourable rate environment saved the day for bankers suffering from the drought in M & A and equity issuance.

As advisors and intermediaries, investment bankers can often have it both ways: earning fees by issuing new paper in bull markets, while offering work-out and restructuring services when boom turns to bust. And as former partnerships turn into public companies, their new stockholders demand some diversification from the notoriously cyclical capital markets. Thus retail financial services and asset management – presumably offering annuity-type income – have been added to the product range of formerly 'pure' investment banks such as Morgan Stanley.

In their constant efforts to leverage their capital base as well as facilitate their marketing efforts, investment banks make full use of another category of products designed to lock in a stream of ongoing revenues. In addition to the products mentioned above with annuity-like revenue streams, bankers have taken equity interests in prospective clients through private equity funds, engaged in so-called merchant banking or bridge loans, and used prime brokerage – providing a range of specialist services to large and active investors like hedge funds.

Another defining feature of investment banking – the creativity of its practitioners – also leads to broadening of the product line as well as providing incremental revenues and the opportunity to pitch new ideas to win client business. A typical quote is that of Richard Ramsden, Executive Director at Goldman Sachs charged with researching the sector:

> "*Investment bankers are continually reinventing themselves. As one area of activity dries up, bankers are remarkable in their ability to reposition and capture the next wave of deal flow.*"

A more colourful comment comes from Karl Dannenbaum, a Managing Director at Lehman Brothers, who describes how product evolution takes place in the turbulent and dynamic world of structured fixed income finance, a Lehman speciality:

> *"We are nomads, dependent on moving and innovating, but our Mongolian plains are called 'knowledge', and we have never yet walked over the same grass twice! What was innovative a few years ago is now being done by junior clerks for a few basis points. You have to be like a shark – swimming all the time to stay alive."*

Mark Garvin, a Managing Director of JP Morgan Chase in London who heads the bank's new product committee, points to another dimension of product evolution:

> *"Innovation is shifting the traditional boundaries between wholesale and retail, and blurring the distinctions between products. Increasingly, our business is about creating value by bundling and packaging products."*

Responding to client demands also tends to broaden the product range. Professor Dwight Crane and his colleagues at the Harvard Business School in their seminal book *Doing Deals* speak of the product creep which stems from a 'self-designing organization' driven by rapidly changing market conditions and opportunities. Philip Purcell, CEO of Morgan Stanley, is quoted as pointing out that:

> *"What makes good strategy is good people on the front line – by osmosis you get the direction you go in . . . products and markets change too fast for McKinsey-type strategy."*[12]

Donaldson Lufkin & Jenrette (DLJ) may well be an institutional case study of a highly successful mid-sized firm drawn inexorably toward the product range of the global bulge group. Citigroup's Managing Director Hans Morris opines:

> *"DLJ faced the classic 'you can't be cute forever' problem. If you're very successful but not very big, there are limits to what you can do for your clients. They focused on equity, research and high-yield debt – a virtuous cycle. But they were no longer 'nichy' and believed they had to be global. It's like the American Revolution: no one expects you to beat the British, and the Americans only won a few battles. Then the client says you have to mount*

a standing army, and you have to adapt in the end. Your infrastructure costs go way up, margins inevitably compress, and you start to feel marginalized!"

The former Chairman of DLJ in Europe before the bank was sold to Crédit Suisse First Boston in 2000, Martin Smith, concurs:

"Investment banks reached a watershed, like DLJ in the late 1980s. There was no going back; you had to grow with your clients, do bigger transactions and offer a broader product capability."

This is the dark side to an ever-expanding product universe. The ebullient creativity of its bankers can push back the envelope with new ideas, but the new businesses may or may not be viable. British merchant banks diversified into the securities business from a highly successful M & A activity in the 1980s in an understandable desire to ensure adequate distribution for the securities issued by their clients. In retrospect it contributed to the hollowing-out of the UK banking sector as the US banks overwhelmed them with superior distributor power and capital. Perhaps with this lesson in mind, Sir Winfried Bischoff, formerly chief executive of Schroders and now Chairman, Citigroup Europe, points out that:

"You don't need to be in the securities business to be a successful M & A house. But the more successful you are, the greater the pressure from your people to go into new areas. You have to be very disciplined, very tough with them."

A contrary view is taken by the advocates of a single – or limited – product strategy, which balances the virtues of specialization with the risk of decay or invasion by others of that chosen niche. I discuss below the special role of M & A advisory in this context.

As indicated by Figure 3.1, pure investment banks have historically earned a premium return on equity (ROE) in the US over their commercial banking counterparts – at least in part due to the factors described above.

Another key dimension of investment banking is the extent of cross-subsidization across products. While they have regularly earned a superior return in aggregate over commercial banks, a number of marginal or loss investment banking products support a relatively small number of highly profitable ones. Figure 3.2 shows one analyst's view of the relative profitability of a wide array of products.

Figure 3.1   Pure US investment banks earned premium ROE over commercial/universal banks during the late 1990s

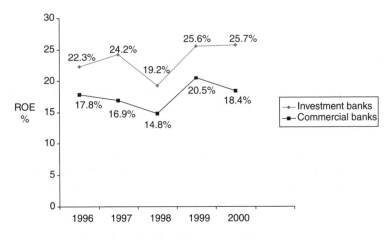

IB: average of Morgan Stanley, Merrill Lynch, Lehman,
   Goldman Sachs, Bear Stearns
CB: average of Bank of America, Citigroup, JP Morgan Chase

Source: Solomon Smith Barney.

Figure 3.2   Cross subsidization supports low return businesses

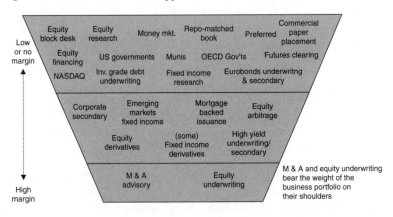

Source: Sanford Bernstein.

Known in the business as 'pay to play' products, such marginally profitable or loss services can include plain vanilla lending, block trading for a favoured client, and equity research. For banks eager to win or retain relationships, offering such products in the hope of winning more lucrative business can be an essential element of a relationship strategy.

As Maureen Erasmus, Managing Director and head of European strategy for Lehman Brothers, puts it:

> *"Some products give you the right to play the game but aren't very profitable – such as cash equity trading, government bonds or providing liquidity, but it's part of the price you have to pay. The issue is whether you have to be a player or a leader in a given business."*

Another means of differentiating the product array is by identifying the buyer within the client organization – specifically the CEO or owner as opposed to the Chief Financial Officer (CFO) or Treasurer. Advisory and equity issuance are assumed to be the province of the former, for whom these are either once-in-a-lifetime or at least infrequent decisions. In contrast, the CFO or Treasurer is usually the decision-maker for debt issuance, lending, derivatives and related products which are used more frequently. Not surprisingly, M & A and equity issuance fees are the highest and most sought after, both for their profitability as well as the proximity they provide to the client and his strategic thinking.

3.1.1 M & A/Advisory

The advisory product not only is the apex of the diversified firms' ideal product pyramid but also, by almost universal agreement, a sound basis for a single product bank.

The value of independent and expert advice is arguably priceless for a CEO suddenly confronted by an unfriendly bid or forced to arrange a complex transaction in difficult market conditions. Under such circumstances, a telephone call to summon a trusted advisor for an immediate meeting at an unseasonable hour is an investment banker's dream.

Such impartial advice has become increasingly valuable as the sector consolidates and many advisors have become part of broadly-based banks which can suffer a conflict of interest by their simultaneous role as a lender or investor. While specialist advisors without such potential conflicts as NM Rothschild and the Lazard Group thus continue to figure in advisory league tables, a growing number of new boutiques, often staffed by seasoned advisors spinning off from these broadly-based banks, has sprung up to satisfy the demand for independent advice.

One of the features of the early years of the twenty-first century has been the splitting of the overall M & A fee among a variety of advisors, including one or more boutiques whose role, as pointed out by Charles McVeigh, Citigroup's Co-Chairman of its investment bank, is

> *"to complement the role of a large investment bank by virtue of the likely strong personal relationship between the CEO and the boutique. The role of the boutique will remain and catch the tail of a number of businesses because of the relatively low incremental cost of adding new products to advisory."*

In this context, the phrase 'You never get fired for hiring IBM' springs to the lips of many of our interviewees. The evidence of customer surveys by consultants such as Greenwich Associates confirms both the durability of such relationships and the criteria used to select and retain such relationships. A classic quotation from such a corporate CFO appears in *Doing Deals*:

> *"Morgan Stanley [their relationship bank] was an easy and practical road to go down. They knew more about us than anyone else. This was not a time for comparison shopping!"*[13]

Table 3.1 summarizes the duration of lead advisory relationships in the US; the larger the firm, the more durable the relationship.

The selection criteria from Greenwich's research are listed in Table 3.2. While M & A fees of millions of dollars can be regarded as over-generous in isolation, they rank only 11th in importance after such subjective factors as an appraisal of the advisor's existing relationship with the CEO and his Board and knowledge of the client.

The stability of these relationships is confirmed by Figure 3.3, which sets out the evolution of the market share of the top three

Table 3.1   Average length of US investment banking relationship with lead bank

	Lead bank
Fortune 500	*(in years)*
Fortune 1–100	13.3
101–200	12.6
201–300	11.4
301–400	9.4
401–500	9.2
Sales Size	
Over $2.5 billion	11.5
$1.0–$2.4 billion	8.9
$500–$999 million	7.0

Source: Greenwich Associates.

Table 3.2 Factors determining mandate for M & A advisory

Credibility with company's CEO and board of directors	
Capability of M & A specialists	
Creative and innovative ideas	
Understanding of company's M & A strategy	39
Understanding of industry	29
Capability of relationship manager	26
Historical relationship	24
Past record in structuring and closing transactions	21
Ability to arrange financing	16
Equity research capability	15
Lower fees	14
Execution support from M & A transactions teams	11
International expertise	5

Source: Greenwich Associates.

Figure 3.3 Big three US investment banks[1] win market share in key lucrative products

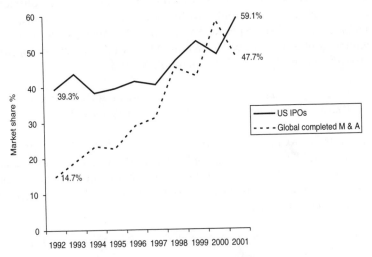

Note: 1. Goldman Sachs, Morgan Stanley, Merrill Lynch.
Source: Bernstein.

advisors in the global M & A fee pool as well as US IPOs. For at least the past decade, three advisors – Goldman Sachs, Morgan Stanley and Merrill Lynch – have not only retained but also actually increased their market share.

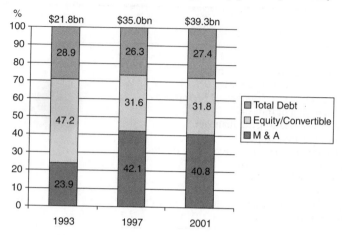

Figure 3.4 Global investment banking fees paid – by product (% of total)

Source: Freeman & Co.

Yet the mountain they must climb to win such relationships has not deterred a host of rivals from the global bulge group. Attracted not only by the lucrative fees but also the proximity of the advisor to the ultimate decision-maker and the ability to influence the award of subsequent mandates, firms like Deutsche Bank, UBS, JP Morgan, Citigroup and Lehman Brothers continued to recruit M & A talent even during the 2001–02 revenue drought. For Citigroup's Bischoff:

> *"We're only number four or five in M & A; we must do better to get that call on Sunday morning from a CEO wrestling with a problem."*

And for those unable to climb the mountain, the failure is a costly one. Cost–income ratios are among the highest in the sector at an estimated 80–90 per cent, with an expensive array of talent required whatever the level of deal volume. Greenwich's polls confirm the lean pickings for second and third tier players:

> *"In investment banking, there is no glory – and not much profitability – in second place."*[14]

The overall fees are indeed lucrative. Figure 3.4 provides a breakdown since 1993 of the global investment banking fee pool – essentially all fees paid by clients for advisory services as well as the underwriting of debt and equity issues. Although fee levels have declined in the US from almost 1 per cent of deal principal in 1987 to less than 40 basis points in 2000, M & A fees still constitute 41 per cent of the total pool.

While there is little debate about the validity of a single-product strategy in advisory, the dialogue continues over the value of diversification for such advisors. With their revenue streams intimately linked to volatile stock market values and the resulting level of CEO confidence, the argument for diversification of revenue sources is added to the functional one of being able to distribute the securities sold as a result of the advice given. We return to this issue in Chapter 11.

3.1.2 Equities

The equity products – primary issuance and secondary trading of equities, convertibles and derivatives written on these securities – constitute a second major product grouping. As indicated by Figure 3.4, in recent years equity issuance has constituted about 32 per cent of the global investment banking fee pool.

The distribution strength of the leading advisory firms explains the high correlation between leadership in M & A and a high ranking in the profitable equity issuance business. Thus the three top global competitors in M & A have maintained a similar ranking in equity underwriting, as indicated in Figure 3.3.

Research from Greenwich Associates in Table 3.3 confirms the relative importance of perceived distribution strength as a selection criterion for the choice of a lead underwriter.

Table 3.3 Factors determining equity book-runner mandate

	Most important (%)
Institutional distribution capability	72
Equity research capability and analyst relationship	61
Credibility with company's CEO and board of directors	34
Skill in structuring and pricing issues	28
Syndicate management capability	26
Historical relationship	24
Retail distribution capability	24
Capable equity capital markets specialists	19
Participation as manager in your past issues	19
Capable corporate finance relationship managers	12
Lower fees or spreads	9
Firm's trading volume in company stock	9
International distribution capability	6
Aggressiveness or bids for 'bought' deals	2

Source: Greenwich Associates.

As an actual profit contributor to the typical investment bank, however, equity issuance is dwarfed by the secondary trading of equities. Figure 3.5, taken from a study by Lehman Brothers, indicates that for a typical bank in both the US and European markets, equity trading accounts for about half of total operating profits. In contrast, equity underwriting fees account for a more modest tenth of the total.

It must be noted, however, that managing an equity issue may lead to additional revenues. Figure 3.6 thus illustrates such revenues derived from secondary fees as well, possibly, as future M & A mandates.

The figure for secondary trading profits masks wide differences between wholesale and retail margins. Figure 3.7 provides estimates of both the trend and level of aggregate margins in Europe and the US.

Institutional or wholesale client trading has exploded since the early 1990s, with turnover increasing largely as a result of hedge fund activity in recent years. The correspondingly higher bargaining power of a diminishing number of large institutions has driven down average wholesale margins in both the US and Europe.

There has been a corresponding surge in retail activity on the back of buoyant stock markets and the equitization of the European retail sector. Margins have remained generous for the banks which can accumulate significant volumes of retail business – the European universal banks with substantial in-house placing power as well as US investment banks with retail affiliates or able to accumulate third party volume through prime brokerage relationships.

3.1.3   Derivatives

The importance of derivatives generically as a profit source reflects both the banks' creativity in product innovation and the wide spreads enjoyed on the more complex and equity-linked products. As indicated by Figure 3.5, perhaps a quarter of total investment banking profits are generated by the explosive growth of derivatives.

For Greenwich Associates, derivatives are

"arguably the most creative, versatile, and influential innovation of recent decades and the most important achievement in modern finance."[15]

In terms of innovation, Figure 3.8 shows how JP Morgan, a leader in most segments of the derivatives business, has progressed from what are now commoditized interest rate and currency swaps to a host of more complex products. The derivatives sector thus comprises a massive

Figure 3.5 Estimated breakdown of US and European investment banking pre-tax profits in 2001

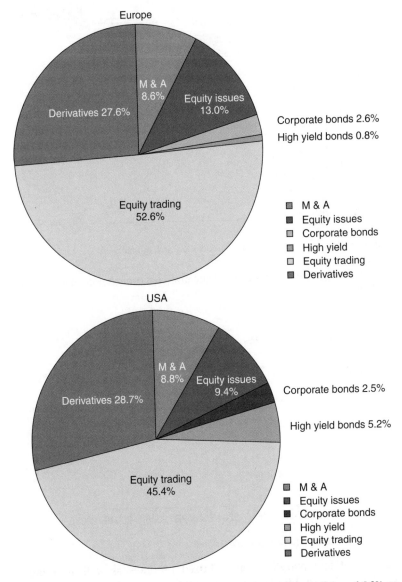

Note: Figures for Europe do not add to 100% because of net estimated *loss* of 5.2% on Government bonds.
Source: Lehman Brothers.

Figure 3.6   The equity issuance revenue multiplier effect

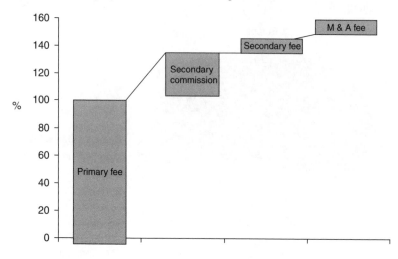

Source: *Thomson Financial Data*, Goldman Sachs Research estimates.

Figure 3.7   Convergence of historical and projected commission rates for equity trading

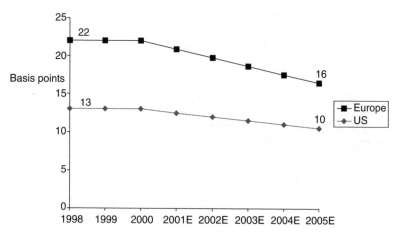

Source: *FIBV*, Goldman Sachs Research estimates.

volume of low margin, commoditized products as well as a much smaller portion of highly profitable and more complex ones.

On balance, however, derivatives yield one of the highest margins of any financial product. The McKinsey/JP Morgan study cited in

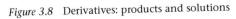

Figure 3.8   Derivatives: products and solutions

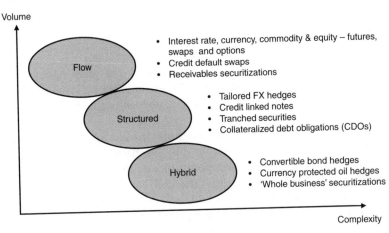

Source: JP Morgan.

Figure 8.4 in Chapter 8 estimates the cost/income ratio on equity derivatives at a modest 20–30 per cent, in contrast to perhaps 65–70 per cent for cash equities.

Starting from simple interest rate and currency swaps in the early 1980s, totally new industry segments have been developed by creative investment banks and their clients. Credit derivatives have exploded from a zero base in 1998 to an estimated $1.4 trillion in 2002 as a straightforward vehicle for banks who wish to unload credit risk and for investors, such as insurers, for the first time systematically to assume these risks. The massive switch of retail and other investors out of equities in 2000–02 into so-called capital guaranteed products – essentially high margin equity derivatives tied to zero coupon, riskless deposits – has been a boon for a variety of banks in the US and Europe who have capitalized on their investors' demand for a guaranteed return of capital plus some upside potential.

Karl Dannenbaum of Lehman Brothers continues his description of the bankers' efforts to create new derivative-based products:

"There's a continual search for new products and solutions. It's like the financial faculty at a university, where hundreds of intelligent and eager minds screen the continually changing tax and accounting rules. And we don't get paid for what we find or develop, not directly anyway, not like consultants. The client takes the ideas and uses them for free, but he pays

you back in doing transactions with you. There is an honour system, and that is where the leverage is."

3.1.4   Debt

Historically a low margin commodity product which has generated profits largely through proprietary trading, the debt sector has expanded in recent years to include conventional loans as well as a host of profitable derivative products associated with the trend towards securitization.

Figure 3.9 plots the average underwriting margin in US debt issuance against its equity counterpart. At only 11 basis points in 2000, it contrasts with perhaps 400 basis points for equities. In a typical year, an estimated 70 per cent of securities issuance is debt against 30 per cent for equity products. In 2001, a bull market for debt issuance, it took roughly ten dollars of debt issuance globally to earn the same absolute fees as for one of equity. The 27 per cent of global fee pool indicated in 2001 for debt in Figure 3.4 thus represents a truly massive volume – roughly \$3.7 trillion in debt issued.

While there is significant evidence that proprietary trading has diminished in relative terms as a profit source, the massive profits garnered in a favourable interest environment by global competitors like Deutsche Bank and Barclays Capital in 2001–02 would indicate that

Figure 3.9   Steady decline in margins on key US investment banking products

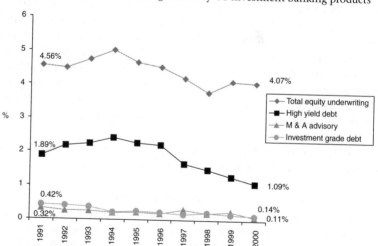

Source: Salomon Smith Barney & Thomson Financial Securities Data Corporation.

the practice is alive and well. A recent study by Goldman Sachs estimates that the share of proprietary trading in the debt revenue contribution has fallen considerably from perhaps 70 per cent in the early 1990s to 60 per cent in 2001 – in favour of structured products like credit derivatives.

Cross-subsidization is particularly rife in the debt sector, where margins on debt issuance and trading as well as the loan product are modest if not negative. As the shift of credit risk to the securities markets gathers momentum in the US and Europe, however, investment banks have earned substantial profits in developing not only the credit derivative product itself but also instruments like synthetic CLOs (collateralized loan obligations) which permit investors to tailor credit exposure to their own needs.

A key management issue in recent years in the debt sector has been the appearance of the plain vanilla loan – known as 'liquidity' – on the debt menu of the global investment banks.

While the 'narrow' US investment banks like Goldman Sachs have always extended credit in connection with present or anticipated transactions, the advent of competitors like Citigroup and JP Morgan with massive balance sheets has emphasized the offer of standard credit facilities as a relationship-development weapon. As we shall discuss subsequently, the threat to the traditional M & A/equity leaders is being taken seriously and seen by many to be a driver for further industry consolidation.

Richard Boath, Managing Director and Head of Financial Institutions in Barclays Capital, describes how the process works:

> "We have risk-adjusted pricing. If you approach a corporate treasurer to establish a relationship, he will usually ask for a credit line. You go to BarCap's portfolio people who will put the deal into their model and tell you what the risk grade and shortfall from the minimum acceptable risk-adjusted return will be. You then try to strike a deal with another product group like the securitization or bond team to subsidize you in anticipation of a possible future debt issue. That unit has to decide whether the risk of winning the business is a manageable one, because they will actually cut a check to the portfolio people."

A parallel trend recently has been the emergence of debt-driven global strategies which rely heavily on the credit as well as debt issuance products to win equity and M & A mandates. Having shed its equity and advisory businesses in 1997, Barclays Investment Banking Unit now defined its mission as becoming the leading European investment bank in risk management and financing. In 2001 BarCap rose to third in European debt issuance and generated operating profits of £685 million.

In Chapter 10, I profile the strategy of Citigroup as well as Lehman Brothers, which has successfully diversified away from a heavy dependence on debt.

3.2   Clients

In a fiercely competitive marketplace, the twin issues of client segmentation and relationship management are top of mind for the investment banks interviewed. Faced with intense competition for the more desirable relationships, the full range of banks is sharpening its focus on a relatively small number of target clients and prospects, while at the same time upgrading their relationship management skills to capture the maximum share of the available fee pool.

3.2.1   Segmentation

For most investment banks, the traditional pyramid based on relative client size or potential attractiveness is the starting point for the segmentation process. For the European market, for example, a recent consultant study provides an estimate of the size of the major national markets based on the 3000 corporations with over $250 million in sales which might constitute investment banking clients. Table 3.4 provides such a breakdown.

Given this data, the response of most mid-sized European banks is to allocate relationship management resources to the segments which are perceived to be most attractive as well as most likely to be won. For such banks, faced with the competition of the global institutions, the second size tier is often given the highest priority. As one senior Scandinavian banker puts it, 'Our target client is someone who isn't the biggest!'

Yet partnering with global competitors for major mandates is a viable strategy for many mid-sized European banks. As Lars Bertmar, CEO of Carnegie Group, explains:

> "We don't have the penetration of the large caps, where the competition from the globals is most severe. We compete with them up to the final pitch, but when the deal is done we are happy to share it. We're 'the best colleague' to the globals – their best local friend. They can't fly in for lunch!"

Table 3.4   Geographical breakdown: corporate and institutional customers by region

	Corporations	Institutions	% of total	% of GDP[1]
UK/Ireland	800	180	27	19
Germany/Austria	600	100	20	24
France	400	40	12	17
Benelux	350	75	12	8
Italy	300	60	10	14
Scandinavia	250	30	8	7
Iberia	200	20	6	9
Switzerland	100	70	5	3
Total	3000[(A)]	570	100	100

Note: 1. GDP is for 2000–01. (A) number of corporates with sales exceeding €250 million.
Sources: Oliver, Wyman & Company, Morgan Stanley Research.

For many such banks with a traditional small to mid-sized corporate clientele, the ultimate rationale of an investment banking activity is to sustain a long-standing relationship when such a client graduates into the capital markets. In such cases the absolute or relative size of the client is less important than his ability to tap the relevant debt or equity capital market.

Figure 3.10 provides a pyramid diagram for BNP Paribas' Corporate and Investment Banking activity, which is typical of many now in use.

Underpinning most such selection processes is the widespread assumption of the validity of the classic 80/20 rule. Our interviewees essentially validated this assumption. BNP Paribas' Bruno Leresche agrees with this rule, but points out that:

"We don't consider the pyramid as static. Our challenge is to move clients up the pyramid, not leave them alone at the bottom."

In its recent strategic review, Merrill Lynch has analysed its client base carefully. Ron Carlson, Merrill's Managing Director and Head of Strategy and Planning for Europe, agrees:

"It's an 80/20 rule with 20 per cent of the clients producing 80 per cent of the profits. It's all about allocating resources to the anticipated return. We have almost the same cost to serve regardless of client size."

Figure 3.10   BNP Paribas' approach to corporate client coverage

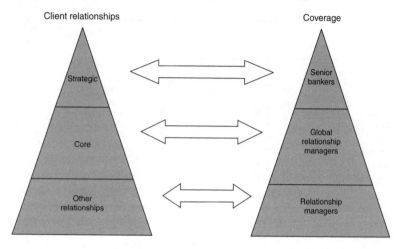

Source: BNP Paribas.

The approach of the global firms is somewhat different from that of the mid-sized players. Its starting point is the likely fee pool – the amount of advisory and issuance fees the client is likely to generate over the intermediate term. Such a fee pool might be estimated at $25–50 million over a three-year period.

This amount is compared with the cost to serve, in the form of marketing and other expenses, to produce an estimated net contribution from the relationship. Given the bank's heavy investment in research, marketing and support costs, there is a natural correlation between the size of fee pool and client priority. The result might be a pyramidal segmentation headed by a target list of several hundred clients and prospects.

A typical example is provided for Lehman Brothers in a recent research report.[16] In 2000 Lehman had relationships with about 1600 companies, but is narrowing its focus to about 850, which are broken down into 'super league' (98 clients), 'franchise' (300 clients) and 'core' (400 clients).

Yet the pressure to grow the revenue base is intense, and the major firms are extending their reach to targets which might have been regarded as more appropriate for mid-sized competitors. Walter Gubert, the Chairman of JP Morgan's Investment Bank, explains the reasoning:

"Given the size of the machine of a bank like JP Morgan, you have to go for a broader range of clients than in the past. JP Morgan now does business with virtually all of the Fortune 1000. There's no question that we'll first deepen, then broaden, this client range. Our engine is powerful: now we need a larger racetrack!"

For the leading specialist advisory firms, the economics are similar to those of the high-volume, high cost global investment bank. Lazard, which regularly figures in the top ten global advisors, is a case in point. As the late Adrian Evans, until his death in 2002 the chief executive of the group's UK business, explains:

"For our model to work, we need clients in the FT 100 category. Unless we do big deals, we can't survive."

Another means of segmenting the client base is sectoral. Cutting across geographical and size criteria is a focus on priority segments selected for a variety of reasons: size of fee pool, natural client base, anticipated profit growth, and strength of one's team. Popular candidates include financial institutions, TMT (telecoms media technology), natural resource firms, public utilities, pharmaceuticals and financial sponsors (private equity and leveraged buy out firms). Sectoral specialization could well justify focus on a second tier firm whose fee pool might well be less than the standard cut-off point.

The importance of sectoral focus historically is underlined by the remarkable success of firms like Goldman Sachs, CSFB and Morgan Stanley who rode the M & A boom of the 1999–2000 period led by TMT clients. In a recent presentation, John Mack, formerly CEO of Morgan Stanley and now of CSFB, estimates that three-quarters of the volume of deals done in those heady years were TMT-related.[17] This view is echoed by a veteran former JP Morgan investment banker:

"JP Morgan built its business around the existing Fortune 500 client base and were quite strong there, but they missed the TMT and financial sponsor segments. You don't make a lot of money from being Bell South's banker, because they don't do many deals, but Craig McCaw [founder of McCaw Cellular Communications] did!"

For both global and mid-sized investment banks, the issue of scale, or scalability, must be addressed. For the former, the question is whether they can adjust profitably to deal sizes which could well be much smaller than in the heyday of the late 1990s. If indeed the billion-dollar tickets for massive TMT deals are largely a thing of the past, can they survive when the client's fee pool is well below, say, $10 million per annum?

Conversely, the mid-sized players may be happy to win such smaller mandates, but can they build a platform of research, marketing coverage and support facilities to meet the competition of the larger banks and still make an acceptable profit?

With reference to US regional investment banking clients, consultant Ray Soifer is not optimistic:

> *"Regional investment banks will never be as profitable as global ones. It costs almost as much to do a small deal as a big deal, and there's been lots of cherry-picking by the major firms."*

I examine these cost-related issues in Chapter 8.

3.2.2   Relationship management

Whether global, mid-sized or specialist, investment banks are upgrading their relationship management skills.

The model for their efforts is that developed by Goldman Sachs and Morgan Stanley which we discuss in more detail in Chapter 5. Under the leadership of co-CEO John Whitehead in the 1970s, Goldman pioneered the concept of marketing to major clients through a team of dedicated marketing professionals termed 'investment bankers'. Later Whitehead and his colleagues introduced the concept of 14 core firm values, one of which is placing the customer first. While other firms have paid little more than lip service to this ideal, Goldman and Morgan Stanley still practise it and have set a standard of client service which is the envy of competitors large and small.

The major challenge they face in relationship management is the product, or silo, orientation of most commercial and investment banks. Traditionally commercial bankers have combined lending authority, their critical product strength, with relationship management responsibility. Such lending officers may or may not be effective calling officers, and they may also fail to bring to bear other products and services to build the overall relationship.

For investment bankers, the challenge is one of specialization and focus on that specialization. Their products are numerous, complex, and often rapidly evolving, while collaboration across product groups is often difficult. The task of interfacing between the relevant specialists and client officers is at best a challenging one. As one veteran banker puts it:

> *"The successful relationship manager is a good GP [general practitioner], who tries to get all the specialists lined up for the client by making the right judgements on timing, personality, etc. If he does his job right, the client will go back to him next time."*

The range of investment banks dealing with this challenge covers the full spectrum of competitors. At the top end, Merrill Lynch's Carlson articulates the problem:

> *"Until now, the investment banker generally focused on the highest margin lines like M & A and equity new issuance. Now investment bankers have to go for everything, derivatives, fx, etc. and must be motivated to cross sell and optimise the total relationship. At Goldman Sachs the partnership mentality has historically positioned them well for this, and this is a top priority for Merrill Lynch. Clearly, line of business and product discipline is critical. The challenge now is to work across products and businesses to maximise overall business potential with clients."*

For global investment banks formed from mergers and aggressive recruitment, the problem is to bring together individuals from different backgrounds and cultures to provide the seamless client service needed.

For mid-sized Continental European banks, the challenge is often seen as cultural. A senior London-based executive with one of these banks explains:

> *"You need to inject a much greater sense of responsibility for originating a revenue stream. The culture is different in our home market; it's not their style."*

One of his colleagues in head office is more optimistic, pointing to the number of senior executives who have grown up in investment banking – a 'varsity' which can sell effectively to large cap clients.

The cultural problem is echoed in Paris by Bruno Leresche of BNP Paribas:

> *"We're working towards a global commitment to the firm culture rather than individual exploits. It's a question of psychology. We have the products and the clients but need permanent pressure to boost teamwork in presenting to clients and cross-selling!"*

In Chapter 11, we explore some of the possible means of surmounting this challenge.

3.2.3 The customer's viewpoint

The voice of the client, whether issuer or institutional investor, is a necessary element in this equation. Rather than undertake what would inevitably be an imperfect survey, I have relied for this input on the work of Greenwich Associates, for decades the industry standard for transmitting this voice to its investment banking clients through its regular and detailed surveys of client views across the major markets.

One major theme of Greenwich's guidance is to improve the intensity and quality of service offered by investment banks, in particular in commoditized businesses such as secondary trading, foreign exchange and investment research. In the low-margin business of fixed income trading, for example, Greenwich's research as indicated in Figure 3.11 indicates the importance of service elements as seen from the client's standpoint.

As Greenwich Associates points out with reference to fixed income clients:

"With the top three relationships, the quality of service almost always takes precedence over price . . . most individual salespersons need to cover

Figure 3.11   Relative importance of fixed income sales factors

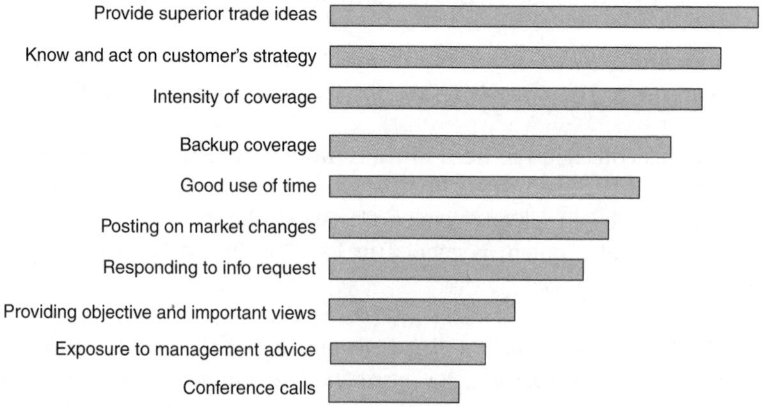

Source: Greenwich Associates.

no more than two–three investors. Salesmen love to add new clients, but it's more important to increase the intensity of existing relationships."[18]

With vast amounts of investment research competing for the client's attention, Greenwich emphasizes the need to be relevant and be read, with lots of follow-on and follow-through to get the client's attention. In the investment banking (M & A and primary markets) arena, their advice is to work for free, be focused and listen, with most aspirants failing to last the course.

A second theme is the superior revenues to be gleaned from being one of the top, if not the leading, provider of a given product. Figure 3.12, for example, quantifies the relative gain in the fixed income sector.

Whether secondary trading, investment banking fees, derivatives or stock brokerage, the story is the same: investors and issuers are steadily consolidating the number of counterparts and advisors. For example:

- 10 per cent of the active institutional investors execute nearly 50 per cent of the total fixed income volume, and 20 per cent execute 80 per cent;
- the typical European investor now uses 13 fixed income dealers, down from 21 several years ago;
- this investor executes two thirds of its total volume with the three most important dealers;
- clients with foreign exchange trading volumes of under $1 billion typically concentrate 80 per cent of their business with their top two dealers;
- typically 70 per cent of derivative trading volume goes to the client's top three dealers.

And in the all-important investment banking fee sweepstakes, 60–65 per cent of the fee pool goes to the company's lead investment bank, with the second winning only 20 per cent of the total. To quote a recent Greenwich Associates publication:

"in investment banking, there is no glory, and not much profitability, in second place ... so do not play to play, but to win!"[19]

As pointed out in the discussion of M & A above, the message has got across, with all eight global competitors targeting a top three ranking in both the M & A and equities sectors.

Figure 3.12   Relative profitability of fixed income dealing relationships

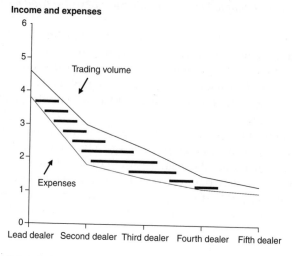

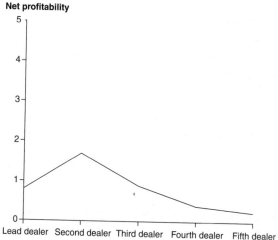

Source: Greenwich Associates.

3.3   Geographical markets

Setting geographical priorities remains a critical issue for all segments of the investment banking world.

For the global bulge group, with global research and client coverage as well as distribution across the leading markets, choices still have to be made. The revenue recession of 2001–02 has focused the attention even of the largest firms on what is essential to sustaining their globality.

Ron Carlson of Merrill Lynch summarizes the results of their strategic review in 2001:

> "You have to offer a full service to clients in the largest financial markets – say the G7 to G10 countries – to provide a competitive global service. The issue is how much further to drill down to do local business. We seek to achieve the highest volumes and revenues with the lowest cost. In a bull market they might generate the returns we seek. But the issue in some locations is when they will come right – in three, four or five years or is it just a long-term hope? We are becoming increasingly demanding that so called longer-term growth opportunities prove that they are able to deliver acceptable returns in the very near term, and if not these investments need to be re-structured."

For mid-sized banks, the issue is more fundamental. In Europe, the 'pan-Euro' concept has been well promoted, but few of the European-based institutions have truly local or embedded operations with, say, more than 5 per cent market share in two or more national markets among the 15 members of the European Union. As Maureen Erasmus puts it:

> "There's a competitive bloodbath in each market with four types of competitors: the US bulge bracket, global European incumbents, the domestic banks and local boutiques. Competitive intensity is more extreme in Europe than the US as evident by greater fee compression and the concentration of fees by the top 8 players. Specifically in the US (in 2001) top 8 firms accounted for 70% of fees whereas in Europe the top 8 account for merely 53 per cent."

Yet Europe remains the preferred growth region for the global firms – as well, of course, as the locally-based banks who generally have no place else to go. Figure 3.13 shows the recent evolution of Europe's share of the global fee pool as measured by Freeman & Co., and a projection for 2005 by UBS Warburg.

Although Europe suffered from the decline in M & A and equity volumes in 2001 more than the US, it still constituted 28 per cent of the global corporate pool in 2001. Almost all bankers continue to repeat the mantra of superior future profit growth in Europe from corporate restructuring, the importation of US products and concepts such as securitization and a broad corporate debt market, and the development of a pension fund sector more closely resembling the US model.

Figure 3.13   Revenue shift towards Europe

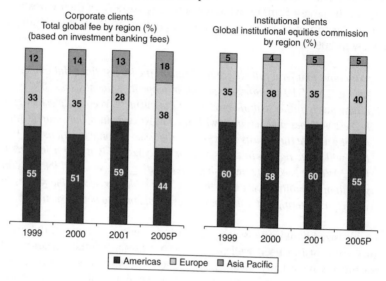

Sources: Freeman & Co. (1998–2001), Leading private industry survey (1999–2001) UBS Warburg analysis.

One of the key themes of geographical expansion has been the need to invest heavily in new markets using profits generated in the home base. We have seen in Chapter 2 how the US banks won market share in key European segments. Why did the same not happen in the case of Japan, which arguably was even better positioned to expand abroad in the late 1980s with soaring domestic profits and league-leading global market shares?

A senior Nomura investment banker offers an explanation:

"Japanese financial institutions are managed from the bottom up on a short-term basis. You can't do that in investment banking; you need a vision from the top. Nomura never had a grand vision, although local people, some more entrepreneurial than others, hired gaijin [foreign] bankers to develop specific businesses. Some, like Guy Hands in principal finance, were successful; most of the others weren't. It's all ad hoc. In contrast, the US investment banks built products and customer relationships, especially with Japan Inc. The export-oriented segment is much more sophisticated than their local bankers, so you find it natural for these companies to talk

to a foreign investment banker. What do they need to do? Build a global business starting in Japan, not London or New York."

Penetrating the US domestic market has been the rock on which countless forays by non-US banks have foundered. The attractions of the market are only too obvious: the 50–60 per cent of the global fee pool paid by US clients, the dominant role of US institutional investors, and the key role played in global M & A by US firms as buyers or sellers. Only CSFB among the US leaders is foreign-owned, the product of a minority interest in the former First Boston Corporation taken as far back as 1978.

Organic expansion has proved comprehensively frustrating to foreign aspirants, while acquisitions have proven only marginally more satisfactory. Sir Win Bischoff, the former CEO of Schroders, articulates the problem of buying a second tier firm which may need to be restructured to add value to its foreign buyer:

"In New York, Schroders made the mistake of thinking that a firm [Wertheim & Co.] ranking in the 11–20 range in the league tables could attract new clients because of the Schroders linkage. Baloney! The US clients had their own relationships and weren't going to shift them for Schroders."

In this context, the success of the US investment banks in penetrating the European and Japanese markets is impressive. The business model of a full product line, global distribution, client coverage and sectoral research, coupled with new product concepts such as securitization and sophisticated derivatives, and the successful operating model we shall examine in Chapter 5, have constituted a powerful cocktail of competitive strengths.

The next few chapters will examine in more detail the competitive response of the European banks most affected by this onslaught. Their business model is in full evolution, with the daily press in 2001–02 replete with announced exits from geographical markets outside their home base, cutbacks in staff, and focus on a more limited client base and product array.

Finally, in this fiercely competitive environment where global and regional competitors are under threat, it is not surprising that even smaller banks with essentially a national franchise have not made a competitive mark outside their home base. Yet a few have, and in Chapter 10 we shall examine the case studies of Macquarie Bank in the global products of infrastructure and structured finance, as well as Carnegie Group as a regional specialist.

4

People: the Role of Culture and Leadership

"This firm has a soul."

– Karl Dannenbaum, Lehman

"There are a lot of 'A' types and 'egos' in investment banking."

– Amelia Fawcett, Morgan Stanley

Investment banking is justifiably regarded as the ultimate 'people' business. It is a magnet for highly ambitious, intense individuals with a high degree of self-confidence and commitment to achieve the best both for themselves and their firms. Establishing a culture which channels their efforts into a firm-wide effort is a major challenge, matched only by the leadership needed to sustain and develop that culture.

What kind of people drive the successful investment bank? It is fascinating to hear practitioners describe their peers. Richard Briance, chief executive of the advisory firm Hawkpoint and a veteran of the London investment banking scene, offers a typical profile:

"Investment bankers are resilient and tough; they are some of the most resilient, toughest and richest creatures on God's earth."

Amelia Fawcett, Chief Administrative Officer (Europe) at Morgan Stanley, concurs:

"There are a lot of 'A' types and 'egos' in investment banking. People are the key; you need to attract, retain and develop the very best people. The enterprise only works if such people feel empowered to work for the clients,

enjoy the firm and work well with their colleagues. It's not an easy task with 58,000 employees!"

Goldman Sachs has become the role model for building and sustaining a successful culture. Peter Weinberg, a member of the bank's Management Committee, confirms the primacy of collaboration:

> *"Investment bankers have assembled a group of very smart, talented, motivated and competitive people. Goldman Sachs has a tough, unforgiving culture but we work together as a team: a team environment, but a tough environment. The key is how people interact – how people work together. The best thing about the old partnership was how people worked together – a strong bond of shared purpose. It has continued as a public company."*

Dwight Crane and his colleagues at Harvard Business School confirmed the unique nature of personal networks in investment banking:

> *"The network in investment banking is distinctive. Because of their role in mediating the flow of assets between issuers and investors, and because of the economic characteristics and product processes, investment banks have an internal network that is unusually flat and flexible ... The complexity of deals, the speed with which many of them are done, and the financial stakes involved, requires a high level of coordination among the people in an investment bank across both function and hierarchical levels ... investment bankers have to be willing to live with the ambiguities, stress, tension and conflicts inherent in a complex and crisis-ridden internal network where everyone is dependent on everyone else."*[20]

Interpersonal relationships in the competitive and volatile world of investment banking are particularly intense and durable. Loyalties to individuals and teams endure for decades despite changes in ownership, structure and job changes. In *Liar's Poker*, Michael Lewis graphically describes the relationships in Salomon Brothers' dealing room in the mid-1980s:

> *"The place [Salomon's dealing floor] was governed by the simple self-understanding that the unbridled pursuit of perceived self-interest was healthy. Eat or be eaten ... The trading floor is a jungle and the guy you end up working for is your jungle leader. Whether you succeed here or not depends on knowing how to succeed in the jungle. You've got to learn from your boss."*[21]

Thus the headlines of the financial press are replete with the news of teams, rather than individuals, leaving one firm for another. And if a key professional leaves to join another firm, chances are that his first call on arriving at his new desk is to his former colleagues to suggest that they join him in his new career.

In this swirl of movement between firms, another rule is evident: the hierarchy of quality is known to all. The ranking of a rated analyst or high-tech investment banker – as well as his approximate compensation package – is fully transparent and followed closely by market practitioners as a measure of a firm's progress or descent. UBS Warburg, for example, has aggressively recruited recently to build its US investment banking business, and many of our interviewees were highly complimentary of the results. Marcel Ospel, the group chairman of UBS, notes that:

> " 'A' people attract 'A' people!"

Yet the resilience of the individual banker can also be detected in the continuity of some teams who have remained at their desks over the years despite traumatic changes in structure, ownership and market cycles. Teams of British bankers from the former Kleinwort Benson have survived the firm's acquisition by Dresdner Bank, two failed mergers with other German banks along with the departure of several hundred professionals, the merger with Wasserstein in New York, and the most recent acquisition and restructuring by the Allianz insurance group.

Such resilience is widespread. Despite its recent well-advertised management and structural turmoil, Crédit Suisse First Boston (CSFB) continues to maintain its high ranking – third in 2001 – in the global fee pool. One of our interviewees notes that:

> "You can put a stake through the heart of CSFB and it still survives."

Perhaps the greatest survivor of all is Lehman Brothers, which I profile in Chapter 10. Having been rescued by American Express in 1984 from a disastrous internecine struggle and a capital problem, Lehman survived several management changes imposed by its new owners, who managed to spin it off in 1994 just before the collapse of the US debt market, which constituted the firm's core business. Yet in 2002 Lehman under the leadership of Dick Fuld, one of the protagonists in the 1984 debacle, has not only survived but also diversified and become a role model for disciplined growth. To quote Lehman's Karl Dannenbaum,

"This firm has a soul. It was scarred by the American Express experience, but the scar made the firm better – more self-aware, more understanding . . . you can't kill this place."

One of the unique dimensions of the investment bank is the extent of built-in conflicts which must be managed. Traders and bankers argue over the 'right' price of a security, functions committing the bank's capital can dispute the level of risk and capital committed, and fund managers and salesmen debate the merits of a security to be placed in a client's account. Overshadowing all is the potential split between a bank's traders who invest the bank's capital and its investment bankers generating fee income.

As the scope of the bank's product range increases, so do the potential conflicts. The advent of credit-driven strategies, with one part of the bank lending substantial sums and another structuring and placing securities for the same client, has been highlighted by the failures of Enron and major telecoms firms in 2001–02.

The literature of the business is replete with the consequences of such conflicts. In his history of Lehman's travails in the mid-1980s, Ken Auletta summarizes the firm's near collapse in a battle between bankers and traders:

"[It is] a story about irreconcilable conflict between two men . . . a poisoned partnership; of cowardice, intrigue and deceit . . . a story of greed for money, power and glory . . . a reminder that human folly, not the bottom line of profits, not business acumen, not 'scientific' management or the perfect marketing plans or execution . . . often determines the success or failure of an organisation."

In less colourful language, Michael Lewis portrays in simple terms the inherent conflict of a salesman in his dialogue with his bankers:

"I faced the same conflict every day selling bonds. If it was a good deal, the bankers kept it for themselves; if it was a bad deal, they'd try to sell it to the customer."

We discuss below the processes and leadership needed to manage these conflicts.

Replicating the 'one-firm' culture of Goldman Sachs is proving difficult for a number of rivals who acknowledge its merits but find themselves up against their own cultural constraints or simply the problems of size and complexity created by growth by acquisition. This issue is particularly acute for European banks faced with the competition of Goldman and its US peers.

A friend at Société Générale's UK investment banking business highlights the cultural difference between the UK and French cultures:

> *"No one has dealt well with cultural differences. The generation which has done the deal is typically not culturally sensitive and able to operate effectively outside its home turf. It's unlike Unilever where national issues have been broken down. It's changing with a new generation used to working in an international context. But there's huge suspicion on both sides as to how to make the business work. The amount of time needed to break down the barriers is not sufficient. Investment banking is about the selling of individual intellectual capacity to put together ideas and sell them. Without confidence in each other it's pretty challenging."*

This is echoed by another British friend at a major Continental bank:

> *"We need a much sharper origination focus. Senior bankers have to look at teams and own clients; it implies a more rigorous selection of clients and a much greater sense of responsibility for originating a revenue stream. The cultural difference is the problem."*

Amelia Fawcett at Morgan Stanley also perceives the differences:

> *"US investment banks are continually reinventing themselves, but European banks have had a fairly protected environment. The process of continuous reinvention is driven by internal pressure, meeting competition and addressing client needs. The question is – do the European banks have that compelling drive?"*

Even some US peers are moving mountains to re-create a one-bank culture. Under the leadership of John Mack, converting the different teams at CSFB to such a culture is a key mantra. Dick Thornburgh, CSFB's Chief Financial Officer, articulates the objective:

> *"Every institution has a culture. All great service companies have a culture of putting the client first, with personal integrity and teamwork at the heart of the culture. I have often expressed the view that investment banking ought to take the partnership form, with all sharing risks together. The most successful firms are former partnerships who retain that culture."*

The universal need is to shift from a product silo or geographic base to customer focus, and this shift has been led by the US banks. ABN Amro among others is passing through a difficult transition period. A senior banker acknowledges that changing from a geographic structure with decentralized management in over 70 countries to a product/client matrix has proven more difficult than expected, in part at least because of the downturn in business volumes.

Institutions moving from a commercial to investment banking format have a particular mountain to climb in creating the appropriate culture for the fast-moving, transaction-oriented investment banking world. Table 4.1 from *Doing Deals* summarizes neatly the differences between the two models.

The classic case of such conflict played a major role in undermining the efforts of several UK commercial banks to establish a successful investment banking business. Philip Augar describes a scene at NatWest Markets which has been repeated on countless occasions when investment banking management puts forward bonus proposals to a management dominated by commercial bankers:

> "The hostility evoked from my senior colleagues shook me badly. Martin Owen [the head of NatWest Markets] was excellent and stood out from them as a person with vision and courage, but he was clearly under enormous pressure from the bank to produce an investment bank on the cheap and was surrounded by bankers who just did not understand."[22]

For many participants, the word 'culture' has become irrelevant in a market where a typical investment banker may have worked for a number of firms, each with its own values and style. Nick O'Donohue, the head of research at JP Morgan Chase and a Goldman Sachs veteran, points out that:

> "There's not a big distinction in culture among the top eight firms. There's been lots of cross-breeding from recruitment. Ten years ago you had unique cultures, but now these cultures have been exported everywhere. We all aspire to the same values."

Several European banks are the product of multiple cross-border mergers. One such senior executive acknowledges the challenge of multiple cultures but points out that the market place sets the rules and behavioural standards, not any particular national culture.

Table 4.1 Management practices in investment and commercial banks

Management practice	Investment banks	Commercial banks
Strategy formulation	Grass-roots strategy formulation within broad guidelines set by top management	Formal top-down process with little room for innovation by people at customer interface
Organizational structure	Self-designing organization that is a flat, flexible and complex network	Tall and relatively rigid hierarchical network with strong departmental boundaries
Management control systems	Measure revenues and profits at aggregate level. Call reports, customer surveys and internal cross-evaluations. Risk control systems for underwriting and trading	Measure profits at aggregate, unit and customer levels. Call reports and customer evaluations. Risk control systems for credit, trading, global interest rate and foreign exchange risk
Bonus determination process	Subjective process by senior managers. Large share of compensation. Highly variable across people and independent of hierarchical position	Little senior management time. Small share of compensation. Little variation across people and amount is tied to level in hierarchy
Relationship management	Senior people heavily involved. Role is highly variable, depending on customer, seniority of banker, firm strategy, etc. Person may be or may not control customer interface and may or may not have product responsibility	Senior people have little involvement. Relationship manager almost always has product responsibility (corporate loans) and retains control of the customer interface

Source: *Doing Deals.*

Bruno Leresche of BNP Paribas agrees that it is values that will define the winners:

"We all have global values which we apply whatever the market conditions. But the winners are those able to translate values into common behaviours that structure an internal relationship model. Companies who care about the internal relationship model achieve not only efficiency but manage to construct an identity and goodwill, something your competitor will never take over when hiring anyone from your organization."

Yet the word 'culture' comes up repeatedly when a firm suffers a blow to its perceived unity. John Mack's departure as Chief Executive of Morgan Stanley, a firm justly proud of its values and unity, has caused some of his former colleagues to raise the issue of reaffirming these values. Donald Moore, Chairman of Morgan Stanley (Europe), discusses his concerns:

> *"Morgan Stanley has the best culture: integrity, team play, respect for the individual, etc. We've always recruited all kinds of people – the best and smartest people. Our culture is not under stress, but rather obscured by the distractions of the Dean Witter merger and John's departure. Have we lost our culture? No, but we have spent a lot less time reaffirming our culture than we should have."*

It is a pleasure to find banks intensely proud of their unique culture and values. Macquarie Bank in Australia is one of these. Its head of investment banking, Nicholas Moore, describes a 'loose/tight' culture which works admirably in the real world as the bank extends its global reach in its specialty businesses:

> *"Culture is at the heart of our business model. It's a way of doing business. Macquarie is a great platform: a good structure, the best people, good pay, etc. But it's just a platform. You need to offer the opportunity for people to do something with it. We call it 'loose/tight'. It's tight when we risk the bank's money, with central controls. It's loose when we say to our people 'Do you want to take the responsibility for a project?' We delegate enterprise and vision. If you do well in Australia and think you can succeed offshore, we say 'We'll support you. We have a bias toward 'yes'!'"*

What kind of leadership is needed to create and sustain such a positive culture?

There is no doubt about its central role, particularly in a period of change and turmoil. Mark Garvin, a managing director who has helped manage four different mergers during his career in London and is in charge of the merger process at JP Morgan Chase in the UK, points out that:

> *"Leadership is critical to success in investment banking – more than ever before. You want the best people and the best can be very demanding. It takes strong, inspirational leadership to motivate teams of driven, highly talented, diverse individuals."*

At the other end of the size spectrum is Lazard, where the same leadership is needed in a different context. Adrian Evans described the need to provide leadership to a small number of highly talented bankers:

> *"Leadership is key to this business. You need someone who can say 'I'm going to do it'. The business does not lend itself to bureaucratic management. It's like a racehorse that needs careful treatment. The issue for advisory firms is how you combine superior professionals with something on top – people with business sense and a strategy."*

Nick O'Donohoe of JP Morgan reiterates a constant theme:

> *"Leadership is critical in this environment. There's a very small number of people who can change the way others work – people like Dick Fuld and John Mack. And the best was John Weinberg of Goldman Sachs, who defined the firm and embodied the values."*

So what kind of people can lead successfully in investment banking?

Probably not individuals from outside the business! Martin O'Neil, a former JP Morgan banker, reminds us of the failures of two highly respected managers in the investment banking world:

> *"It's like the media business; if you're not from that industry, you just don't get it! Look at Jack Welch and Warren Buffett: both made major investments in the business and failed."*

One of Welch's few failures at General Electric was the collapse of Kidder Peabody. Having acquired its first investment banking interest in Kidder, GE Capital was finally forced to liquidate it following a series of executive changes. Buffett's admirable efforts to instill a sense of stock-holder value at Salomon Brothers in the early 1990s met the implacable opposition of the firm's revenue-generators. One is also reminded of the unsuccessful efforts of American Express to impose similar 'management principles' at Lehman Brothers.

For such otherwise successful generalists, leading a team of investment bankers must resemble 'taking a bunch of squirrels for a walk in a park', a phrase attributed to David Scholey, formerly CEO of SG Warburg!

What does work is the player-manager – a unique individual who combines professional qualifications as a real investment banker with the 'something else' to which Adrian Evans refers. Citigroup's Sandy Weill is thus widely viewed as such an icon: a unique individual who understands the business from the ground up, has successfully acquired and integrated a host of investment banks and brokers, and has the judgement and vision to lead a large and complex firm from the front.

How do they do it? What is the formula for success which escapes so many would-be investment banking leaders?

BNP's CEO Michel Pebereau, who managed the challenging Paribas merger, receives praise from one of the Paribas executives closely involved in the merger process:

> *"There's a high level of emotion in a merger. Pebereau managed these emotions. He was transparent and honest, not cosmetic. He really looked for best practices. He could say 'stop the BNP machine and be pragmatic. Swallowing them [Paribas] would destroy their effectiveness'."*

Martin Smith, a veteran investment banker who built DLJ's European business, describes the formula admirably:

> *"The problem in investment banking is that the leadership tasks tend to go to the best investment banker, who may or may not have the best management skills. The biggest revenue-generator is put in charge of the shop. You need a player-manager, as in football, to have credibility.*
>
> *There are three dimensions. First, it's rare for management in investment banking to create a sense of direction and vision. Second, you have to have the skill of being able to manage a highly-incentivized group of people in what is seen to be a transparent fashion. This breaks down when people haven't put enough thought into doing it properly. Thirdly, the leader must be trusted – someone who can operate politically and deal even-handedly with all the vested interests and keep his personal position subordinated to those of others. It's a rare skill!"*

The football analogy can also be used in a negative sense. Robert Colthorpe, a managing director of Société Générale who has worked for three separate owners, agrees that effective leadership is a rare skill:

> *"Lots of people think they're good at it but they're not. Organizations are bad at picking the right people with cross-cultural skills. Outside of Goldman*

Sachs and Morgan Stanley, very few investment banks have done a good job of building a leadership group. The bigger firms' leadership tends to act like a football manager: 'Our centre half isn't working; let's hire another'. They haven't built a group that works well together. At Goldman and Morgan Stanley there are a number of good people who spend time managing the business and making sure people behave. People know what to expect: the norms of acceptable behaviours. It's not cuddly, but it's easier to manage when you have these norms."

Even at role model Goldman Sachs, Peter Weinberg feels there is room for improvement:

"Leadership at Goldman is evolving. For years, investment banks were unmanaged. We're trying to professionalize management and have hired a senior professional from General Electric to help us become better leaders and managers. Now our leaders have a cultural role – to promote teamwork, intensity and integrity. But you still need the commercial focus; Hank Paulson [the CEO] spends a lot of his time with clients."

And the need is not just for one leader but for depth in leadership. As Amelia Fawcett at Morgan Stanley puts it:

"Leadership comes in different ways; it's not only the guy who is on the podium. For truly successful organizations leadership must take place at every level of the organization. The danger is not only having one leader who can disappear, but also that you're not getting the very best out of talented people. Leadership at every level should result in maximum client satisfaction, enhanced market share and strong financial performance."

At Citigroup, the world's largest financial institution, Sir Win Bischoff agrees that the team approach is essential at the top:

"At Schroders, I thought that 6,500 people was too big! At Citi, the challenge in many respects is easier. If you have a strong, energetic CEO like Sandy Weill and a top team of around 50, with the CEO in contact with perhaps 500–600 additional executives, you hardly miss a beat if you lose a few people."

Perhaps a unique dimension of leadership in investment banking is the use of co-heads either at the top of the organization or at a divisional level. While such co-heads may be simply an interim solution while the candidates fight it out for the job, in Goldman Sachs it has been refined to a science. Beginning with the legendary 'two Johns' – Weinberg and Whitehead – who assumed the role of co-CEOs in 1976, the firm has successfully blended complementary skills, such as trading and advisory, to achieve a more integrated management structure.

As Whitehead explained in an earlier interview:

> *"Co-chief executives don't work for everyone, but they did for us. Two leaders can do twice as much as one – if they work effectively together. John [Weinberg] and I had worked closely together for years; we had the same vision but completely different strengths and weaknesses. When the succession to Gus Levy came up, we were the leading candidates. Rather than fight for the top job or split the firm up between the two of us, with one of us managing half the business and the other the other half, we decided we'd like to run the whole thing together. It worked because we talked every day. We had occasional disagreements – usually about people – but we talked them out between ourselves."*[23]

Finally, as in any business, there are horses for courses: specific individuals who are more effective in some circumstances than others. Thus many of our interviewees pointed out that John Mack was the ideal choice to turn around a firm like CSFB which had strayed far from the 'one-firm' ideal as well as allowed its cost base to skyrocket.

By the same token, the arrival of Bruce Wasserstein, a master rainmaker and charismatic leader, was probably appropriate for Lazard, which had been suffering from a drain of senior talent and internal friction.

5

Structure and Process

"The organization chart isn't very interesting. The key is how people interact and work together."

– Peter Weinberg, Goldman Sachs

(Creating the appropriate environment for the unique investment banking culture is a central challenge for any bank regardless of size or business model.) Can there be 'one bank' or many? How can one allow for the flexibility needed to adapt to market opportunities? And how can a large and complex organization focus its resources to achieve the nirvana demanded by the intense client focus described in Chapter 3?

(The starting point for this adventure is portrayed in *Doing Deals*. Written in the mid-1980s, this book still forms the basis for the 'one-bank' model shaped by Goldman Sachs and Morgan Stanley. To quote the Harvard Business School researchers:

> "To a large extent, investment banks are self-designing organizations . . . Because of the complexity of the business and the speed with which it changes, strategy is formulated largely below the most senior level through a grass roots or bottom-driven process . . . The self-designing organization gives people throughout the firm a high degree of autonomy . . . Investment banks have an internal network that is unusually flat and flexible . . . [It] requires a high level of coordination among the people in an investment bank across both function and hierarchical levels."[24]

The investment banker's world has not changed much since the mid-1980s except to become even more complex and challenging. Globality, a wider array of increasingly complex products, consolidation into larger firms, the conversion of former partnerships into stockholder-owned companies – all these and other factors have raised the bar for a successful investment bank in the twenty-first century. Nick Paumgarten, a former First Boston investment banker now with JP Morgan Chase, summarizes the evolution of the past two decades:

> *"The business has totally changed; it's not the one we grew up in. We used to be 35 professionals in First Boston and we were the number one underwriter. Will technology solve the numbers problem? No: these firms are too damned big. Now we've evolved into a gigantic military operation. It can't be any other way."*

Yet the ideal operating model shaped by Goldman Sachs and Morgan Stanley still centres on a 'one-bank' structure with processes to support it. Mark Garvin of JP Morgan Chase speaks for several of today's new global powers:

> *"In our mergers we have consistently espoused and implemented a fully integrated model. The 'one firm' mindset is implicit in the vision."*

The new management team at CSFB, which has passed through extraordinary turmoil since its origins as First Boston, articulates the same view on structure. For CEO John Mack, 'one bank' has become a mantra. CFO Dick Thornburgh confirms that

> *"We use a single relationship manager. The focus is on client relationship management. In investment banking, it's a much more complex challenge than in equities, with a more complex product array, a longer gestation period between deals, and multiple decision-makers. Goldman Sachs is still the role model for this relationship process."*

But getting there from here is a steep mountain to climb. It is steepest for former commercial banks whose traditions, decision-making structure and organization model are centred on a relationship manager equipped with the formidable credit weapon. Not only is such an individual often ill equipped to market the investment banking products, but he is usually reluctant to give up his power as lender and gatekeeper to serve the overall relationship. The former

JP Morgan undertook the painful transformation early in the game in its efforts to transform a leading wholesale commercial bank into an investment banking competitor. Martin O'Neil describes the process:

> *"Bringing together in one organization your investment and commercial bankers is an agonizing process. There are two ways: JP Morgan's long, slow process or a brutal machine-gunning of your top commercial bankers. It's not an easy process in either case."*

Yet one by one, commercial banks in Europe and the US are following JP Morgan's lead by going through the painful process. Société Générale in France was an early convert in Europe by creating its Corporate and Investment Bank (CIB) unit in 1995. As its deputy head Patrick Soulard explains,

> *"Investment banking is not a standalone business for Société Générale. Since 1995, one 'senior banker' sells all the products. We were one of the earliest to do so in Europe."*

Others have followed. Among the banks interviewed, HSBC integrated its investment banking unit into the commercial banking entity a few weeks after our interview with investment banking head Stephen Green. A new management team in ABN Amro brought together the two elements to create its Wholesale Client Services division, whose strategic role is to support the asset-gathering function.

Yet the integration process for such banks is rarely a smooth one, with the merger often having more form than substance. William Connelly, head of investment banking at ING Barings, describes one form of compromise:

> *"Investment banking reports to the head of the wholesale businesses. Our role is to generate value added in areas such as high yield debt, acquisition finance or primary equity deals. We'll never be fully aligned with the corporate group; investment banking will always have its own role. It's like the Olympic circles – I try to enhance and enlarge the overlap."*

Other banks with a commercial banking origin reject the 'one-bank' model. In Sweden and other Nordic markets, the preferred organizational structure splits the M & A and equities businesses into a separate entity with its own corporate structure, compensation system and management processes.

Do the benefits of attracting and retaining investment bankers offset the conflicts which may arise with the commercial bankers who control the client relationship and the credit product?

For Enskilda Securities, the highly successful investment banking subsidiary of Sweden's leading corporate bank SEB, the answer is clear. Per Anders Ovin, Enskilda's CEO, believes:

> *"There is no internal competition in the SEB group. Both kinds of structure work: there are pros and cons for each. People focus too much on organizational issues so they can look good. It's all about doing business. If you have the right culture, all the boxes don't matter."*

His rival Göran Björling, Executive Vice President and head of Handelsbanken Markets, the investment banking division of Svenska Handelsbanken (SHB), tends to agree:

> *"We have a pretty sophisticated system developed over 30 years. The SHB branch has the client responsibility, and we have the product responsibility for advisory and equities. Revenues are split with the branch or the region. But we see the debt and equity groups growing together over time, and I can see common client management for the equity and debt businesses."*

Yet it all depends on your organizational point of view! A former SEB corporate banker paints a different picture:

> *"In the past SEB tried to merge their investment bank and commercial banking units. The war went on for years. Finally management knuckled under and the investment bank was spun off to become an independent entity. The investment banking people argued that they needed independence because of client confidentiality, but in addition they were worried about their compensation programme being pulled into the bank. Their view was that the 'the revenue is ours; the commercial bank contributed very little.'"*

In the context of a 'self-designing' organization which is constantly changing to meet market conditions and where change is driven more by client and market-facing professionals, the traditional organization charts beloved of commercial bankers have little meaning. This is just as well, as few of the banks from which we requested a sample organization chart were prepared to give us one! The only one prototype we could identify in the publicly-available literature is that profiled in Figure 5.1, provided by Professors Roy C. Smith and Ingo Walter of the Stern School of Business at New York University.

While an experienced investment banker might recognize this structure, the untutored outsider might be a bit lost. We have therefore provided Figure 5.2 on the basis of our own research and interviews. This is a much simpler diagram which illustrates the principal revenue-generating units and key functional relationships.

We were assured by many friends that organization charts in investment banking are not worth the paper they are printed on. As a consultant working with banks on their structure, Norman Bernard is quick to point out:

> *"An organization chart is meaningless in investment banking. Bankers feel they don't need such a chart. They're a very, very driven community which doesn't take easily to reporting relationships and lines of hierarchy. They focus on the object of the exercise: the client and the deal."*

Peter Weinberg of Goldman Sachs elaborates:

> *"The organization chart isn't very interesting. The key is how people interact and work together."*

Client coverage is the litmus paper test for the 'one-bank' structure. Client surveys as well as the Goldman Sachs model demand a single relationship manager – the 'investment banker' in a traditional investment bank – who figures in the upper left of Figure 5.2. His key marketing role is to build a close relationship with the client CEO and other executives, to develop a deep understanding of the client's strategy, to identify marketing opportunities, and to bring to bear the skills and resources of his firm to exploit these opportunities. In addition, he may also personally have responsibility for providing corporate advice to his client.

In an increasingly complex and competitive world, he has become a specialist in the client's particular sector – health care, telecoms, and so on. As Donald Moore of Morgan Stanley puts it:

> *"It is difficult for a team leader to be effective without a deep knowledge of the sector."*

Yet the massive size and complexity of some of today's investment banks creates challenges for this remarkable individual which, in the

Figure 5.1 Structure of a full-service securities firm

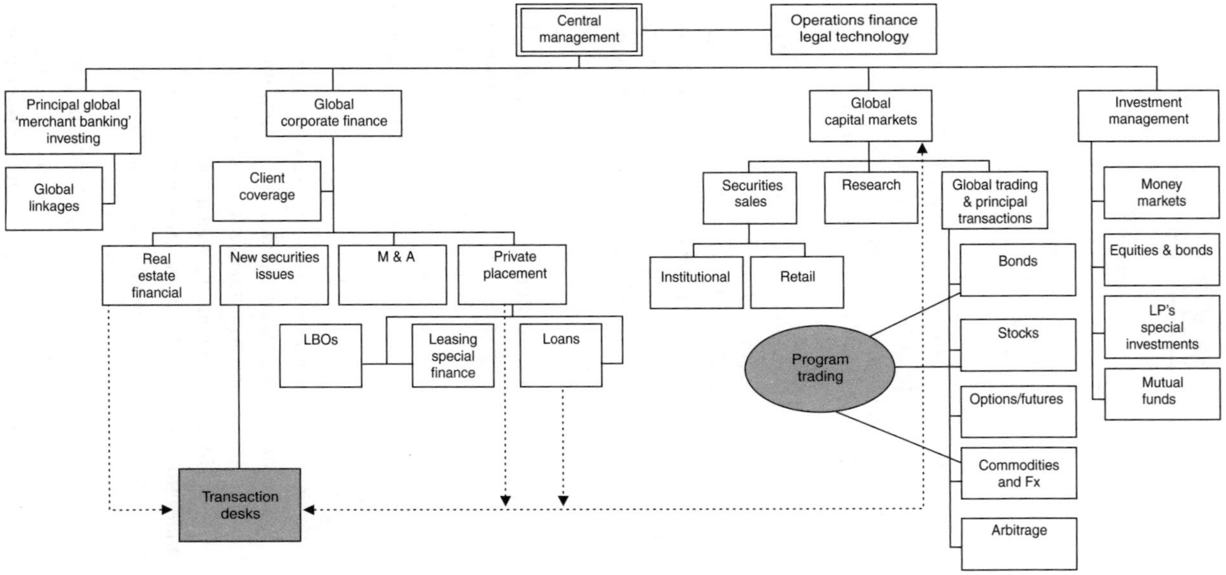

Source: Professors Roy C. Smith and Ingo Walter, Stern School of Business, New York University.

Figure 5.2   Key revenue-generating functions in investment banking

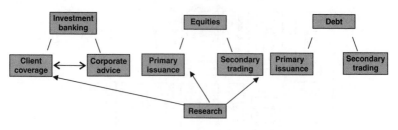

view of many, are too much for any one individual. However intense, competent and hard-working he may be, can he deliver effectively the full range of his bank's products and services?

Walter Gubert of JP Morgan offers a pragmatic solution:

> *"It's too complex a world to put everything on the shoulders of one individual. Our account manager is the 'CEO' of this firm for his client. He doesn't need to know all the products in detail. What he does need is the clout and judgment to act as CEO and say 'We're going to do this' and work with a team of people with the relevant skills – to run the team and give recognition to team members for their contribution to that relationship. The challenge is that you need very high calibre people."*

The same approach is followed by others. For Patrick Soulard, Deputy Chief Executive Officer of CIB at Société Générale, his senior bankers also act as 'CEOs for the client', each handling from six to ten clients. Graham Clempson, formerly head of European Investment Banking at Deutsche Bank, agrees that a single account manager is the right solution, but stresses the challenges:

> *"The issue is to have that single relationship manager truly have the relationship as well as the authority to control delivery – which isn't easy. But you also need a culture in the firm which rewards teamwork and meets individual profit goals. In Deutsche Bank there's been a remarkable change: there used to be separate businesses: now they're run as a single business. You create a virtuous circle, a sense of common purpose as Goldman Sachs has created."*

As the largest financial institution in the world, with a strong heritage from acquisitions in both corporate and investment banking, Citigroup has evolved a unique model of dual coverage. Rather than jam these individuals into the classic 'single banker' mould and risk losing talent from predecessors Citibank and Salomon Smith Barney, Citi has assigned a commercial banker from Citibank and an investment banker from Salomon Smith Barney to co-lead each client relationship. As Hans Morris, Managing Director in Citigroup's Corporate and Investment Banking (CIB) group, explains:

"If you plot on a graph the two dimensions of frequency and seniority of client contact, you see that the most complex, high-value products like M & A and equities are in the northeast quadrant and the standard commercial banking ones in the southwest one. No one individual is qualified to cover all of them. Citibankers are excellent at their job, but very few can get into the top end and dialogue with the CEO as an investment banker can and our investment bankers don't have the credit knowledge of the Citibankers. Why take excellent goalies and insist on making them centres? We believe we offer a better relationship when everyone plays their position.

We found that trying to decide who's in charge was a pointless exercise. It's too emotional a question and frankly it doesn't matter. We're partners on the client working together, doing joint reviews, etc. It's an A plus from the client if both of the two are stars but an F if they're both weak, and frankly only a C plus if one is excellent and the other poor. We think both organizations now understand this, and the improvement in quality and congeniality is noticeable."

Will it work and produce the seamless client relationship desired? Robert Statius-Muller of Greenwich Associates acknowledges that universal banks like Citigroup have turf problems and cultural issues:

"It's great to have both an investment and commercial banker under the same roof, but in practice you may need separate account officers for the two product areas, with the seller matching the buyer in the client organization – i.e. the investment banker selling M & A and equity products to the CEO and the commercial bankers selling loans and bonds to the Treasurer and CFO. I haven't yet seen the individual equally competent in selling all products at all levels. What happens in practice is that each has his own bias and tends to neglect the products he's not comfortable with."

Whatever client coverage model is used, the challenge of successful execution is a major management preoccupation. Arguably those organizations still effectively separating commercial and investment banking products have the most difficult mountain to climb. But even the 'one bank' advocates like Citigroup and JP Morgan Chase must create a working environment where information and relationships are shared freely and on a proactive basis.

JP Morgan Chase is one of the few global banks to provide a client relationship coverage model. Figure 5.3 illustrates how the investment bank relates to other parts of the group.

In this context, a culture of strong internal communication is a key success factor. Nicholas Coulson, a NM Rothschild investment banker who began his career at SG Warburg, describes the different operating environments:

> *"I've always worked for investment banks with a strong culture. SG Warburg was the original, seminal culture. The penalty for withholding information was death. It was an 'archival' culture: everything was committed to paper. In contrast, others are like supermarkets: you get a desk and a telephone and are expected to produce. Success in investment banking is leveraging off information to get a competitive advantage. At Goldman Sachs voice-mail communication is compulsive and compulsory. In the more hostile cultures you either withhold information or trade it for something of value to you."*

Figure 5.3   JP Morgan integrated client relationship model

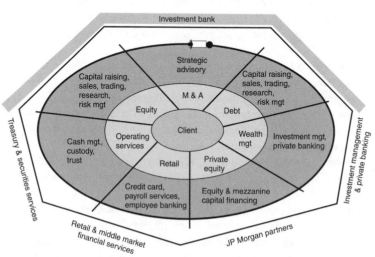

Source: JP Morgan.

Friends at Citigroup and JP Morgan Chase describe the massive investment in information technology designed to bring client-relevant information onto the banker's computer screen which had either not existed before or had remained locked in people's minds. As Hans Morris explains:

"We've found that the key is to share information, not to reinvent the wheel. We've spent a lot of money to develop on-line systems for customer information. It's a critical competitive advantage. A lot of the information simply hadn't been available."

Yet the risk is pointed up by a friend at JP Morgan Chase:

"Now everything is on the computer; all information on the client is there. But there are some things you can't put on the computer. I use the telephone!"

A universal issue for all investment banks is to bridge the gap between product specialties and relationship managers. The generic business challenge of matrix management is sharpened in this business because, as Norman Bernard of First Consulting explains:

"Most investment bankers are specialists, with long-standing client relationships. When it comes to execution, it often boils down to the availability of a small number of people with very specific experience."

Having built DLJ's investment banking business in Europe, Martin Smith agrees:

"Increasingly everybody becomes a specialist. You have to develop a matrix structure."

Getting these specialists to emerge from their product silos and collaborate in a marketing role is not a simple task. Nicholas Moore, head of investment banking of Macquarie Bank, acknowledges that his bankers are better at products than relationships:

"Client coverage has been relatively chaotic to date. Our people are technically focused; we need to be on the cutting edge. It's a cost of the culture. Technical people don't manage relationships well. But we're moving to more of a relationship focus and away from product, along industry lines. There's no formal gatekeeper, but in each industry group we expect people to know all the clients."

Across the world in Stockholm, Lars Bertmar, CEO of Carnegie Group, another highly successful mid-sized bank, agrees:

> "We have no single relationship manager. We're pretty bad at relationship management, but we're getting organised! We're very entrepreneurial and are all financial engineers. Hopefully, a client comes along and wants to buy something!"

Client focus is a challenge even for the most successful banks. Donald Moore of Morgan Stanley acknowledges:

> "In 2001 we went back to a Banking Department with a focus on clients, supported by a slimmed-down M & A function. The goal is to improve client focus – giving the client what he deserves – a service differentiated from the other investment banks."

Richard Ramsden of Goldman Sachs reiterates the challenge as seen from the analyst's point of view:

> "There's a need to move away from a product to a client focus. Take a good fixed income client who calls up the bank's equity department and is told 'Sorry you haven't given us anything'. It's an insane thing to do! It's what the firm as a whole gets which is relevant. Firms like CSFB are merging their fixed income and equities businesses in an effort to break down the product silos and improve cross-fertilization. The clients demand it!"

In the struggle to break down these barriers and focus on marketing a range of services to a single client, one senses that the European banks are having a more difficult time than their US counterparts.

A number of our French and German interviewees pointed to a cultural reluctance on the part of their colleagues to represent the entire firm to a client. Patrick Soulard of Société Générale cites the need to develop an in-depth approach to clients as one of his team's principal challenges. His bank's corporate and investment structure, which is typical of a number of other European banks, is shown as Figure 5.4.

At BNP Paribas, Bruno Leresche describes the challenge:

> "To sell down the product chain is more than a question of team playing, it's a basic marketing principle. The clients don't belong to the métier [business unit] but to the bank. When you do a big deal, it's a magic moment for the client, and the time to do some marketing along the chain

Figure 5.4 Société Générale: corporate and investment banking organization chart

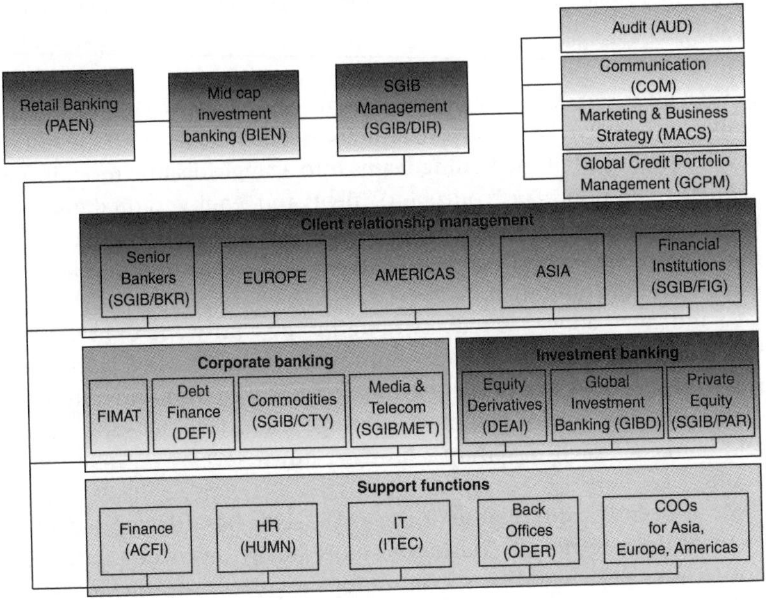

Source: SocGen.

of products, rather than sit down and celebrate your own success or go off to the next client!"

When the geographical dimension is added to this client and product matrix, the global investment banks face a three-dimensional challenge which has defied even the most sophisticated and talented management teams. Marcel Ospel, who has guided the former Swiss Bank Corporation through a series of well-executed mergers to become one of the leading global competitors, acknowledges the enormity of the task:

"It's a great challenge for UBS to achieve that ideal of 'Thinking globally, acting locally'. You need some things centralized, while other decisions can be made regionally. Distance does play a role in operating in markets like Asia; being in London and New York isn't enough. You need a strong regional management and oversight. Doing business in France and Germany is different, and they're right next door to each other! As clients become more

sophisticated, the issue of being able to deliver a whole business will become more important. One person representing only part of the firm simply can't do it alone."

In their efforts to develop a flexible, client-focused approach, investment banks have evolved a number of structures which have stood the test of time. Bringing all of the trading teams into a single dealing room is one standard solution. The concept of debt and equity capital markets teams, for example, brings together investment bankers originating the transaction with the salesmen and traders who have responsibility for pricing and distributing it.

As indicated above, effectively merging the equity and debt product specialists under one head also improves communication and client service. And Goldman Sachs' past use of co-CEOs from different ends of the business is also designed to bridge the divide between traders and bankers which has almost brought down several US investment banks.

Most recently, the collapse of the TMT sector has driven a redeployment of these teams into businesses more likely to generate business – not an easy task given the specializations involved. As Amelia Fawcett of Morgan Stanley explains:

"You shift people around as the business changes. We've asked people in investment banking to shift to equities or private banking, depending on the need or opportunity."

Throughout the interview process, however, our sources kept returning as an ideal format to the partnership structure as evolved by Goldman Sachs and Morgan Stanley before going public in the 1990s. Richard Ramsden, of Goldman's research unit, notes:

"An investment bank is the most perfect form of socialism. The firm is run largely for the benefit of the participants, with the profit pool based on a share of revenues with some contribution to the outside stockholders!"

As we discuss in the following chapters, compensation and other issues are being addressed in the context of this partnership ideal.

72   Investment...
The deca...
sation a...
packag...
For
num...
vic...

6
Compensation

"The lunatics have taken over the asylum."
– Norman Bernard, First Consulting

"If you can't explain the reward system, you're dead."
– Amelia Fawcett, Morgan Stanley

The issue of compensation lies at the heart of an investment bank's efforts to attract, motivate and retain the unique human skills which are its raison d être.

Quite simply, money lies at the heart of the relationship between investment bankers and their firm. As *Doing Deals* puts it:

"Based on a contract, investment bankers are trading quality of life for money . . . ego and greed drive investment bankers – making money and doing big deals."[25]

The author of *Liar's Poker* describes vividly the emotions of a Salomon Brothers investment banker at bonus time, when the variable amount of his compensation is revealed:

"One climbed through the ranks at Salomon by pointing to a chunk of money at the end of the each year saying 'that's mine – I did that . . .' On 1 January 1987, [the year] 1986 would be erased from memory except for a single number: the amount of money you were paid. That number was the final summing up. Imagine being told that you will meet with the Divine Creator in a year's time to be told your worth as a human being. You'd be a little edgy about the whole thing, wouldn't you?!"[26]

of the 1990s both demonstrated the importance of compen-
d raised the issue of whether *any* business could afford the
s being offered in an unprecedented bull market.

an investment bank like Lazard so totally dependent on a limited
ber of high performers, the difference between a virtuous and
ous circle is a narrow one. As Adrian Evans of Lazard put it:

> *"You do good deals and attract good people, or the reverse; a 'knightly brotherhood' which hopefully works in a virtuous circle. For Lazard in 2001, it didn't work. We couldn't attract good people. They know the economics and ask 'Will I be able to make enough money?'"*

Fortunately for Lazard, Bruce Wasserstein was recruited to head the group and proceeded to reverse the outflow of talent from the New York office.

The explosion of compensation levels which peaked in 2000 produced an outpouring of concern from managements as well as academics and consultants. Norman Bernard of First Consulting puts it graphically:

> *"The big issue in investment banking is that the lunatics have taken over the asylum; they have hijacked the income stream. In a commercial bank, the institution owns the clients; the banker is an agent. With investment bankers, on the other hand, it's like breeding racehorses. We've taken some Arab stallions and bred them to be very tough-minded, voracious characters, and it's only natural that they've hijacked the income stream."*

Professor Emeritus Sam Hayes at the Harvard Business School raises issues both of public policy and management control:

> *"Look at people like Mike Millken [a former head of the failed Drexel Burnham] making more than $500 million! How do you balance payouts with human capital – the whole genius of the firm – and the owners of the capital? The current generation of management has you by the short hairs; they can walk, and do. There's no allegiance to the firm. You exploit it for what you can get. Now human capital is treated as a variable cost; people are fired at the slightest indication of a downturn. Part of this is a stockholder value mentality, but it's also because the firms' overheads are so big. They're seriously in danger of foundering unless they can throw some babies to the wolves."*

But it is top management which must face the immediate consequences of having not only paid historically high levels of bonus but also committed themselves to fixed amounts of future payouts – in violation of the old partnership creed of tying payouts to actual performance. Donald Moore of Morgan Stanley expresses a typical view:

> "Compensation expense has gotten out of control. The revenues can't justify it. It is getting realigned in 2001–2002. The solution is variable and stock-based compensation."

At CSFB, where a new management team is addressing both the downturn in volumes as well as the heritage of substantial guaranteed future bonuses, Dick Thornburgh summarizes the strategy:

> "The goal is that no long-term contract will be based only on the individual's own performance. Everyone has to believe in the importance of firm performance. We got rid of the two–three-year deals and unlimited upside packages. We had to build a company rather than a group of independent contractors."

The solution to all these and other compensation problems is almost universally seen to be a very simple one: return to the old partnership concept with a single basic profit pool doled out on the basis of perceived contribution to the firm. The research for *Doing Deals* in the mid-1980s produced the remarkable observation that all of the many firms interviewed used a single bonus pool across the firm as the basis for their compensation plan.[27] As most of the old partnerships are now public companies with no prospect of returning to the good old days, management's answer is to re-create the partnership concept to the extent possible in terms of compensation formulae.

The 'magnetic north', or ideal model, of virtually all of our interviewees is the partnership concept developed by Goldman Sachs in the decades before its public flotation in 1999. The concept is blissfully straightforward: a single bonus pool awarded to a large eligible pool of professionals and allocated at least in part on the basis of perceived contribution to the firm. The awards are based usually on three levels of contribution: to the firm as a whole, to one's unit, and for personal achievements.

The process is inevitably an subjective one, but it is based on an exhaustive gathering of written inputs not only from the individual banker but also hierarchical superiors, peers and subordinates. Hence the phrase '360 degree review'. While complex, the process is perceived to be both open and fair: all involved have their say, and the result is hopefully accepted as a fair compromise.

So much for theory! The practice, or execution, is something different. Even Goldman Sachs itself admits to the difficulty of executing its own model. Peter Weinberg points out:

> "Our review process is quite time consuming, but an effective review system is essential. For example, we expect our Managing Directors to be reviewed by a significant number of people at all levels in the firm. Commercial skills and overall effectiveness are, of course, critical elements in our assessment of compensation, but other aspects like being a team player, mentoring junior colleagues and engaging in activities that reinforce our culture are just as important."

A host of problems await the top managers, who must find a balance among the highly articulate claims of different product, geographic and client groups. The year 2001, for example, was a banner year for fixed income, while for most firms M & A and equity origination stagnated or collapsed – primarily due to market forces beyond the powers of individual bankers or firms. Richard Boath of Barclays Capital describes the dilemma:

> "The big issue in a full service investment bank is balancing compensation among functions, especially in a year like 2001. It was unique in that the profit pool was smaller than it had been since 1994, and in 2001 the fixed income people shot the lights out. When function heads get together to debate the 2001 split, the fixed income guy is likely to say 'I've made 80 per cent of the profit' and demand a share accordingly. Violence will then ensue, with the fixed income guy saying to the others things like 'Why do you need to pay millions to your tech analysts and all those other equity research people?'"

Whatever the outcome, however, it must be perceived to be fair, and the basis for the split explained to all concerned. At Deutsche Bank, Graham Clempson explains:

> "The key is to be seen to be fair – that's actually more important than the amount. It's a game of relativity, of fairness."

And the process must be communicated across the firm. Amelia Fawcett of Morgan Stanley agrees:

> "If you can't explain the reward system, you're dead. It's partly the 360 degree process, partly client feedback, and a function of the tripartite

split between results of the firm, the division and the individual. People often
don't get it – for example, when one division has a bad year and a banker
thinks he had a great year. It's a question of communication. You need
basic rules for everyone – in particular to link people to the firm's success."

Inevitably the Goldman model is modified to suit a bank's philosophy
and circumstances. At Citigroup's CIB, which blends career investment
and business corporate bankers, Managing Director David Bowerin
describes how two different compensation frameworks for corporate
and investment banking will interface:

"There are two separate compensation models for [investment and corporate
bankers] with each benchmarked against the relevant market. Similarly,
there are product-specific compensation frameworks for specific markets
like F/X; if they exist, we acknowledge them. For relationship managers in
corporate banking we use as balanced score card to assess performance."

Does it work? His colleague Hans Morris sees progress being made:

"I'm not sure there is much difference in philosophy between the two.
Execution is more important than strategy. Everyone agrees that the
360 degree approach is necessary with an honest response, a team frame-
work, reward for individual performance, and obtaining the right behav-
iour with a result that's reasonably fair and transparent. But it's hard to
make it work. Over the past four to five years we've improved the process
by concentrating on making it work well. For example, we use a specialist
outside the individual unit who authenticates the process so it's not political.
We banish advocates from the committee! But every year we adjust the
knobs to improve it and take out biases. Now people believe in the system –
it does produce the right behaviours. But it took three to four years to
get here."

The global firms agree that cultural values must support whatever
compensation system is in place. Mark Garvin of JP Morgan Chase
expresses the bank's philosophy:

"The distinctive feature is culture; anyone can make money available! You
need to motivate people – to instill in them the belief that the firm's vision
and values will create superior performance. It's about behaviours,
attitudes and values. It sounds soft, but it's not; we say the soft stuff is the
hard stuff."

His colleague Walter Gubert elaborates:

"The compensation philosophy must be in sync with the business philosophy. Ours is 'One firm, one team'. You pay for performance, but the end result must reflect the firm's overall results at least as much as your team's financial contribution. At JP Morgan, we first look at the individual's contribution – a complex process. Perhaps 10 people might opine on an individual's contribution – a committee will evaluate his or her contribution to the organization. This is then calibrated with how well the firm has done. In a tough year like 2001, when there can be a big divergence between the two, we have to recognize that people who only want to be paid on their own individual or team results should go elsewhere."

Fixing the amount of the bonus pool itself is a challenge for many. Banking historians will recall the failure of efforts by Warren Buffett as a major investor to introduce into a troubled Salomon Brothers in the early 1990s a bonus plan which established the pool as a percentage of earnings above a minimum return on the firm's equity. Faced with the prospect of not receiving what they regarded as a fair share of the revenues in a bad year for the firm, key traders in the firm revolted, and the plan was put aside. Mr Buffett later sold his interest in Salomon.

Considerably better results were obtained at about the same time in Sweden when the present Carnegie Group was spun out of the former Nordbanken, a commercial bank which had to be bailed out by the Swedish government during the regional banking crisis. Lars Bertmar, its chief executive and author of the formula, explains how a similar formula worked – essentially fixing the bonus amount at 50 per cent of net earnings before bonus but after a minimum risk-free return to outside stockholders like Nordbanken:

"You have to look at the two sides of the same coin. When the formula was established ten years ago, Nordbanken suspected that if we had a good year, the investment bankers would take everything, and if it was a bad one they would take more! Our people wanted to protect their downside, and they think the formula is fair. 50/50 isn't rocket science! We had a huge level of distrust as a background, but now both sides think it's fair."

The concept of a single bonus pool for all wholesale bankers in a typical European universal bank has spread well beyond the global leaders who espouse the 'one-bank' concept. Patrick Soulard of Société Générale describes a pool which includes both commercial and investment bankers who make up the bank's Corporate and Investment Bank (CIB):

> *"We've created a partnership structure in CIB for about 50 top executives on a global scale. The top five people in CIB manage the partnership, which is renewed every year and shares a profit pool."*

And Svenska Handelsbanken is moving in the same direction in its Handelsbanken Markets investment bank. As Göran Björling explains:

> *"We replaced an ad hoc system a few years ago to create a more transparent one. Bonuses are small by global standards, but for a group of key professionals – say 10% of the staff – there is a common bonus pool, a partnership concept, part of which is paid in cash and part locked up for several years in SHB stock."*

Finally, ABN Amro has incorporated a bonus element in a recent package for its professionals in its Wholesale Client Services business which ensures that relevant professionals will receive an agreed bonus element if certain plan targets are met over a four-year period.

But for most European banks, who essentially share a commercial banking heritage, both the concept and level of an incentive package of the same order of magnitude of its US counterpart constitute a bridge too far.

A senior friend at one of these banks observes wistfully:

> *"Partnership? Head office is allergic to any form of profit sharing. Top investment banking management has tried four times to introduce one."*

Several European banks maintain different compensation levels for professionals based in head office as opposed to London or New York. As Bruno Leresche of BNP Paribas points out:

> *"Bonuses are based on métier [business line] and geographically. People understand when packages differ by market; things aren't the same in Paris and New York. We don't use 360 degree but rather evaluate the individual. Does it work? There's no manifest crisis!"*

And even when a commitment to pay performance bonuses exists, the process can be an agonizingly slow one. A London-based senior investment banker with experience in working for two European universal banks describes the forces of resistance:

> *"At one bank, there was the problem of hiring a star and watching him fail. There was resistance by the incumbents as opposed to 'How can we make him succeed?' Buyers of investment bankers start by saying 'Pay what it takes', but management resists increases as the size of the business grows. There's lots of institutional resistance – 'Why pay him that?' Any system with high variable compensation will focus on the big numbers. Strains develop in the system unless the allocation is fairly managed. It's difficult to develop the necessary systems such as 360 degrees; you need a lot of management process to make it work."*

The fallback position for such banks is a separate profit and loss statement for the pure investment banking function. Among other things, this enables bonuses to be paid to traders and other professionals in line with local standards but without contaminating the pay structure of the commercial bankers, who are essentially paid on a salaried basis. Such structures exist in units like ING Barings, which has its own P and L and essentially manages its own bonus system, and did at least until recently in HSBC until the merger with its commercial banking counterpart.

One of the pitfalls of the bonus theory was revealed in mid-2002 when HSBC's decision to reduce bonuses significantly after a weak year in 2001 triggered an exodus of senior equities bankers and analysts. The *Financial Times* quoted an unnamed banker as saying:

> *"Anyone who can leave is leaving. HSBC made a huge miscalculation by not paying its bankers bonuses and now they are watching the franchise crumble in their hands."*[28]

Management's response was that paying no cash bonus for 2001 was based on the poor profit record of the equities functions.

Among the myriad variables which go into the complex process of allocating bonus amounts is the need to keep on board valued professionals, especially in buoyant market conditions when job offers proliferate. A friend at Nomura Securities recounts his experience:

> *"The key is the group leaders who pay to keep their people. It's not scientific, and it's not just on the basis of performance. There are lots of*

*variables – what the guy can earn elsewhere, whether you can buy
loyalty, etc."*

Nick O'Donohoe of JP Morgan Chase, who must manage the compensation of hundreds of equity analysts, suggests that job function should be a major driver of incentive compensation:

*"You have to distinguish between producers and managers. I don't believe
in the producer/manager; you are either one or the other. When people are
promoted, they find it difficult to give up the support of production. It's
a real problem in investment banking: it's OK for a manager to have client
contact but it's much more difficult to figure out how he adds value. You
should have a partnership culture for managers, who should be paid more
on firm and division-wide results. Their reward is prestige and power."*

So how can the perceived conflict of interest between investment bankers and their outside stockholders be resolved? The answer, once again, lies in the magic partnership concept. By effectively re-creating the partnership in the context of a quoted public company through the issuance of stock options or equity lock-ups, management believes it can not only ensure individual commitment over a period of years but also increase alignment between outside and inside stockholders.

Thus a major portion of today's incentive compensation is paid in the form of such equity instruments. The phrase 'rich but illiquid', which used to be applied to Goldman Sachs partners before the flotation, also applies to them and their counterparts from similar firms which have gone public. A major strategic goal of Lehman Brothers' management is to increase the present level of over 30 per cent of Lehman stock held by employees. A friend at Morgan Stanley notes wryly that, with 95 per cent of his net worth tied to Morgan Stanley stock, his motivation is assured for years to come!

The same view is echoed by the management of today's global bulge group created by recent mergers. Sir Winfried Bischoff of Citigroup agrees with his peers at Lehman:

*"The goal should be to maximize the amount of shares in the hands of our
people. 10 per cent ownership [the portion currently held by Citigroup
employees] is simply not enough. Paying cash doesn't foster togetherness.
For the lower ranks it's hard to create that loyalty. Equity is the way to do
it. You lock them in for a few years. The top people can be bid away, but
the others will be reluctant to leave that money on the table."*

What if you can't offer quoted stock or, worse, the stock goes down in value? The former dilemma is a major challenge for family-owned firms or partnerships such as NM Rothschild, Cazenove or Lazard. Thus one of the first decisions of Bruce Wasserstein in early 2002 on taking over the reins at Lazard Group was to announce that a portion of the group's equity would be made available to its key professionals, while Cazenove has announced the future dissolution of its centuries-old partnership, with a flotation to take place before April 2003.

For NM Rothschild, which remains in the hands of its eponymous family, the lack of a quotation is a constraint. As Nicholas Coulson explains:

> *"NMR doesn't offer equity, which puts more stress on the cash component of reward. For most investment banks, the more they earn the more they get in stock; perhaps half of the total these days is in stock. You can use phantom stock, but that doesn't match what the US investment banks can offer. Does it hamper NMR's ability to attract and retain people? It's hard to say, but look at our record of earnings and increased market share!"*

Such phantom stock is the solution of firms like CSFB, which are wholly-owned by larger, more diversified financial service entities whose stock price might not reflect closely the efforts of its investment bankers. Such stock is usually based on an earnings formula tied to the investment banking entity's actual performance and pays out over time in cash or parent stock.

The peril of reliance on quoted stock, of course, is that it may rise or fall for reasons which might or might not be linked to actual investment banking performance. Thus the substantial fall in 2001–02 of Deutsche Bank stock, arguably linked to the weak performance of the bank's retail/fund management division, provoked such unhappiness among its investment bankers that options awarded at prices above the current market will be repriced downwards, albeit in smaller amounts.

To conclude, as in the case of structure as well as other dimensions of the ideal investment banking model, there is widespread agreement among the industry leaders on best practice in compensation strategy. Establishing a single bonus pool tied to actual performance, and issuing as much stock as possible to employees, are the twin goals of such a strategy. As usual, the devil is in the execution, which is clearly one of the most challenging of all issues for bank management. And, also as usual, there are banks such as the mid-sized European competitors who have not yet totally bought into this wisdom.

We return to these issues in the final chapters.

7
Risk Management

"The key risk is someone who deliberately or unwittingly fools the system."
> – Lars Bertmar, Carnegie Group

"The biggest risks are those we don't know about."
> – Richard Ramsden, Goldman Sachs

(Risk is a central issue in investment banking.) Yet the original outline for this book did not contain a chapter heading on risk management for the simple reason that previous efforts to query banks on this issue elicited a standard, defensive response to the effect of 'Not us; we don't take risk'.

(But on reflection I decided to include it. The litany of investment-bank-related disasters is too long and repetitive to ignore. On learning of my intent to explore management issues in the sector, a number of friends rolled their eyes and opined that the book might be a very short one: were investment banks managed at all, or were they simply a hedge fund out of control!?

There certainly is a pattern of risk-driven collapses and massive losses which can be attributed to a failure in risk management. During the past two decades alone the list is a long one. First, there are the self-inflicted wounds: for example, the collapse of Drexel Burnham in 1990 and of Baring Brothers in 1995 as well as near-failures of Lehman Brothers in the mid-1980s and Kidder Peabody in the 1990s.

Then there are the client losses which can be attributed to the zealous efforts of investment bankers to invent new ways of making – and losing – money: the Procter & Gamble/Orange County derivative losses in the mid-1990s as well, arguably, as Enron-type structured finance losses more recently. And of course the heavy losses which shook but did not sink individual investment banks: private equity/merchant banking investments at the beginning and end of the 1990s, the massive fixed income losses taken in 1994 when US interest rates suddenly went north, and the speculation on Russian government bonds which went horribly wrong in 1998.

The job description of an investment banker may imply a natural exposure to market volatility, but the results of the past few decades alone add a bit of zest to the roller coaster ride. Unprecedented floods may occur once a century, but in investment banking the cycle seems a bit shorter – perhaps once every four years.

Even the paragons of investment banking have suffered their share of setbacks. Readers of Lisa Endlich's excellent history of Goldman Sachs will learn the detail of such crises in the firm's history as the collapse of Penn Central in the late 1960s, the arrest and subsequent jailing of its head of risk arbitrage in the 1980s insider trading scandal, the firm's financing of Robert Maxwell in the late 1980s, and substantial dealing losses in London in 1994 which created a crisis of confidence for the bank's new management team.[29]

In the interview process, our fears of put-down denials and defensive responses proved groundless. Our interviewees were more than prepared to address the risk management issues. What did they regard as the risk categories of most concern? How happy were they with the new risk management tools now available? And how did they see future risk trends?

Before addressing these issues, we need a few definitions and statistics. Investment banking risks come today in three basic flavours: credit or counterpart (the risk of loss of principal and interest); market (adverse movements of interest rates, equity prices, or currencies); and operational risk (a 'catch-all' basket covering human and systems failures which drive, directly or indirectly, serious losses). We address each in this chapter.

What can we learn from the available database? The trends offer a mixed picture. First, investment banks – at least in the US – are increasingly relying on proprietary trading – essentially risking the firm's own capital – to sustain revenue growth. As indicated by Figure 7.1 below, the proportion of revenues from this source has climbed from 20.1 per cent to 26.0 per cent over the period 1998–2001. The good old days when an investment bank made most or all of its profits from providing advice or executing transactions as agent are long past. The good news is that these incremental trading risks have been balanced, at

Figure 7.1 US investment banks replace fees/commissions with principal/trading income and asset management fees

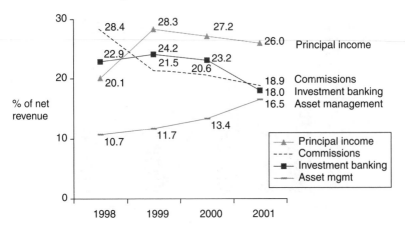

Source: Company documents and Fitch.

least in theory, by more reliable income streams from private banking and asset management.

Secondly, widespread agreement has been reached on the measurement of market risk through so-called VAR (value at risk) models, which quantify on the basis of historical price movements the possible principal loss – usually up to a 99 per cent probability – due to adverse market action. Perhaps in response to the increased transparency thus generated, since 1998 the US investment banks (among others) have significantly reduced their VAR risk as measured as a percentage of tangible equity capital. Figure 7.2 tracks this ratio over the period 1998 to 2001.

Thirdly, investment banks appear to have achieved improved risk/reward ratios in market risk as measured by the ratio of trading revenues to VAR. Figure 7.3 expresses this relationship as the multiple of such annual revenues by asset class against the average VAR amount for that asset class. Among other insights, this indicates a higher average relative reward in recent years as well as the superlative gains made on taking equity risk.

Increased transparency in market risk and reward, however, is not the whole story. Investment banks remain exposed to risk of loss in their lending, block trading, private equity, and underwriting as well as proprietary trading businesses. Breaking them out is not the simple task it usually is for a commercial bank, for which the average annual loss provision on its loan portfolio is a commonly accepted measure which covers the bulk of its risk-generating activities.

Figure 7.2 Trends of VAR/tangible equity capital ratio for major US investment banks, 1998–2001

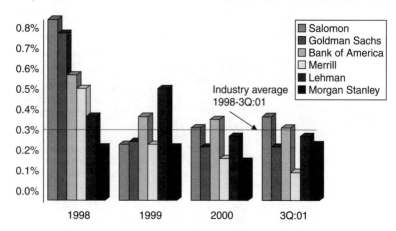

Source: Sanford Bernstein.

Figure 7.3 Risk-adjusted dealing profitability of global investment banks[1]

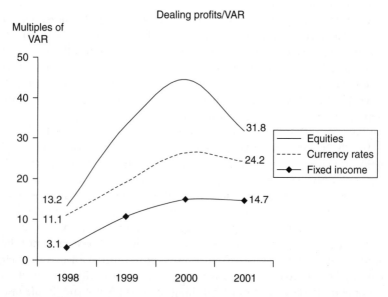

Note: 1. Sample includes CSFB, Deutsche Bank (CBS division), JP Morgan Chase (Investment banking division), Lehman, Goldman Sachs (GCM division), Merrill Lynch (CICG division), Morgan Stanley (Securities division), Citigroup (CIB).
Source: UBS Warburg.

Our interview series gives a useful insight into management priorities and concerns.

Credit or counterpart risk, which is usually associated with commercial banks, has assumed a key strategic role with the advent of new global competitors like JP Morgan Chase and Citigroup prepared to use their balance sheets to build relationships. The traditional bulge group leaders such as Goldman Sachs are well aware of the challenge of what they term 'the provision of liquidity' – in other words, lending as a stand-alone product. As Peter Weinberg of Goldman Sachs sees the issue:

"We use our capital aggressively on behalf of our clients. Typically, we don't provide unfunded commitments unless there is a clear take-out, for example, in the case of bridging loans and some commercial paper facilities."

Amelia Fawcett of Morgan Stanley agrees:

"Some companies will make you 'pay to play', but you need a balance between providing bridge finance and other deal-related lending, and simply paying to play. If you're doing a complex, highly confidential M & A transaction which requires bank lending, in the past you'd go to a bank which would then syndicate it at the risk of breaking confidentiality. Now we can lock it up by doing the entire deal internally and then selling it on after the deal is public."

Her colleague Donald Moore emphasizes the client need for pure advice:

"Let's make sure we have a good credit function and build a product capability in the context of the overall securities business. However, it is not clear how big a business this needs to be. We are told by some very big corporates that 'We don't want a conflict of interest when we need to call on you to advise us'."

While universal banks like Citigroup and JP Morgan Chase have been criticized for so-called credit-led strategies which offer low-cost credit to win relationships, they vigorously defend their position. Hans Morris of Citigroup offers a most articulate view:

"Credit is a big issue; we talk a lot about it. The credit portfolio is run as a business, and the head of risk management reports directly to Sandy Weill, who is intensely risk-averse! We don't use credit as a leading weapon; we only apply the balance sheet to a client and have fired the client

when it's only a credit relationship. Credit is only an enzyme for the client relationship."

For banks with a heavy overhang of problem loans, a credit-led strategy is not the issue: to the contrary, less is more! The inheritance of bad telecoms and Enron-related exposure at banks like JP Morgan Chase has both damaged the brand and hampered the merger process. A *Fortune* article in 2002 demonstrates how different views on credit risk can exacerbate a sensitive merger process:

"The tension between Chase and Morgan wasn't about cultures: it was about risk. Their merger brought together two diametrically opposed views of risk management, one swashbuckling (Chase), the other hyper-disciplined and scientific (Morgan). Clearly they could not co-exist, and in the immediate aftermath of the merger a battle erupted internally . . . seven of the top ten global credit risk managers from JP Morgan have since left the company."[30]

Credit risk can also be a distraction from the basic business of running an investment bank in Europe. For a senior friend at Dresdner Kleinwort Wasserstein, the principal risk challenge is to work through a substantial portfolio of problem loans – and at the same time to convince their insurance owner, Allianz, that the basic business of corporate and investment banking is a sound one.

In sum, credit risk is both a practical as well as strategic issue for investment banks. In the view of bank consultant Ray Soifer:

"Well over half – say 60–70% – of risk in the universal bank is credit risk. It's not managed as well as it could be. There's always been the temptation to underprice. The traditional investment bank now has lots of credit risk, but they lack the credit culture."

With regard to the all-important issue of **market risk**, most of the banks interviewed are relatively comfortable both with the management tools available and also with their ability to achieve the desired results. A typical view is expressed by Stephen Green, main Board director and head of investment banking at the highly conservative HSBC:

"Investment banks are in the business of managing risks. You mediate in markets. And it's not just market risk: look at the settlement risk issue after

September 11 in New York. What do you do when suddenly the volatility element of your model goes through the roof as it did then, and your VAR soars. Do you cut back your exposure? It's a judgement call."

Judgement is the phrase used by many of his peers. As Walter Gubert of JP Morgan explains:

"We use lots of controls and different risk management models, but ultimately what matters is judgement."

For Amelia Fawcett of Morgan Stanley, which is highly regarded for its management systems, there is a cultural dimension to risk control:

"The front line of defence is a system of management controls and proced- ures. The issue is whether we have a robust control system which is under- stood by everyone, along with independent validation. It gets you a long way to feeling confident. Do you have a culture where someone sees something that doesn't look right, and where that someone can go to a senior person and say 'There's something wrong here' and get action? You'll always have a bad apple. The question is whether you can find it quickly and fix it and put robust controls in place to ensure it doesn't happen again."

Her colleague Donald Moore emphasizes the role of culture as a risk deterrent:

"Leeson [the trader who sank Barings] couldn't happen in Morgan Stanley. There are all sorts of checks and balances, including systems and people who understand the business. People all around him would be watching."

Another highly regarded risk manager, Peter Weinberg of Goldman Sachs, also emphasizes the role of experience and judgement. In his view:

"Models are important but only one part of the puzzle. Systems tell you what the risks are, but you need adults to understand them. In 1994, we all were surprised by market movements unforeseen by historical data analysis."

Graham Clempson of Deutsche Bank agrees that progress has been made but that the struggle is an ongoing one:

"The sophisticated investment banks have a good handle on market risk. We've learned a lot about market volatility and incorporated it into our

VAR models: they're tested to the full. If we have sleepless nights, it's for two reasons: a greater degree of correlation across business lines than anticipated, and the quality of risk management in counterparts with a broad portfolio of businesses."

For Société Générale, a global leader in the highly volatile world of equity derivatives, diversification is the key dimension of risk control. Patrick Soulard explains:

"We've strengthened our risk management function since the BNP battle and reduced our risk profile by exiting some emerging markets. We're not a prisoner of VAR models. We basically look to diversification in the key derivatives function, with over 40 separate businesses controlled by one senior risk manager."

The quality of professionals on the trading floor and their risk controllers is a key variable for Sir Win Bischoff of Citigroup:

"There are two key dimensions of risk: methodology of risk control and the judgement of your people. At Schroders we didn't want to take much risk because we couldn't attract the best traders. It's perfectly legitimate to go for more risk/reward if you're comfortable with it."

His colleague Hans Morris offers a somewhat less sanguine view:

"The 'science' of risk management is, in my experience, regularly subordinated in execution to the quality of judgement and appreciation that some change in behaviour will obviate all of your models. Looking back 10–15 years, you see similar situations: mortgage service rights, the IO [interest only] strips from mortgage loans, Russian bonds, equity 'portfolio insurance', etc. In each case, the big financial institutions lent money against just about any collateral and built a large book of risk. When you run your VAR models out to two or three standard deviations, and see manageable exposures, your comfort is based on some anticipated range of behaviour. But then it does [change]; now we have [with the Enron example] ratings change with unimagined speed – so you have a rapid collapse of the house of cards and incredible impact on liquidity. No one model can actually predict the future scenario. What's remarkable is the resilience of capital and the ability to firms to recover."

Eileen Fahey, who has responsibility at the rating agency Fitch for US investment banks, focuses on process and structure:

"While VAR exposures are a measurement of risk appetite, it is riddled with assumptions and difficult to view as a pure number. Trends in VAR are more revealing. What's more important and revealing is to determine potential risks through stress testing. But similar to VAR, the tests are dependent upon historical assumptions. Stress testing is also a means of aggregating risk across the organization and allows a discovery of new potential sources, both for individual sectors as well as the aggregate."

Yet an iconoclastic voice on the use of these models can still be heard. Consultant Norman Bernard is one of these:

"There's a willing acceptance of risk when dealing with statistical models. Banks try to avoid risk by managing out the underlying causes, while insurers accept it within limits. Derivative risk is different. The volatility numbers are used to make a prediction of likely future prices based on historical ones. These historical prices don't reflect today's underlying risk, just the market's view in the past. Only someone like a credit officer digging into the details can get close to the real risks. Don't tell me that such real risks are reflected in the price. Just look at the massive volatility of Russian securities in 1998 and Enron in 2001 when the market suddenly understood the real risks."

The category of **operational risk** in its various forms has captured the attention not only of practitioners and owners but also of regulators. One of the issues which has driven the extended debate over the introduction of Basle 2 (the proposed new guidelines for regulatory capital) is quantifying what many practitioners feel is inherently unquantifiable.

For investment bankers, however, the risk is quite real. Of all operational risks, that of the rogue trader stands out for many of our interviewees. Echoing Amelia Fawcett's concern, Maureen Erasmus of Lehman Brothers places operational risk – the effectiveness of the organization and its culture – at the top of her list of risk control priorities.

In Scandinavia, all three of our interviewees highlighted the issue of fraud. 'People not sticking to the rules' is a major concern of Enskilda's Per Anders Ovin.

Lars Bertmar of Carnegie agrees that human error is the most serious form of risk:

"The key risk is someone who deliberately or unwittingly fools the system. I don't lose sleep over market risks, which are well-managed. But

every now and then an individual does something he shouldn't do. It's seldom because he is a criminal, but because he gets into a pattern he can't get out of. It happened in Norway in 1994 and we lost a lot of money."

Another Scandinavian head of investment banking, Göran Björling of SHB, has unhappy memories of a rogue trader and espouses the need for a cultural defence mentioned by Amelia Fawcett:

"Collusion within the bank is a concern. Fifteen years ago SHB suffered big losses from people fooling the system. There's no complete protection except when the organization is so successful that any employee would reveal any sign of such collusion."

A different form of operational risk is damage to a firm's reputation, either due to actual losses suffered or as a result of behaviour which undermines the bank's brand and value system. Thus reputation risk is top of mind for Goldman Sachs' Peter Weinberg:

"For Goldman Sachs, reputational risk is number one. To quote [former co-CEO] John Whitehead, it's the hardest to get and the easiest to lose."

For essentially a single-product firm like Lazard selling independent advice, reputational risk is understandably dominant. As Adrian Evans made clear:

"You can go broke in our core business if you screw up a major deal and get sued for a multiple of your fees. There's also reputational risk if you take on the wrong kind of client."

A veteran British merchant banker, Robert Colthorpe, adds a qualification:

"If you trade off your name, maintaining image is very important, but if you have a broader base, it's less important. Thus Goldman Sachs wasn't really hurt by the Maxwell affair [involving diversion of pension funds], but Morgan Grenfell lost lots of credibility after Guinness [market manipulation]."

How well do investment banks manage their aggregate risk exposure? There are mixed views. Mark Williams, the head of McKinsey's investment banking practice in London, believes there is room for improvement:

"Getting an integrated view of aggregate risk is tough. Only a few investment banks can get a picture in real time of risk to, say, the top 50 financial

counterparts. When a trading desk has to re-calculate total credit exposure, you don't have time to do it manually. Some commercial banks are streets ahead of the investment banks in this respect, and some investment banks take days to make lending decisions – a tortuous process. Other banks may have credit limits in place, but if they want to stop all payments to a given counterpart, as was the case of Barings in 1995, their systems fall short."

Nicholas Hayes, a former Citibanker and head of the international practice of RMA (formerly Robert Morris Associates and now The Risk Management Association), agrees that there is more to be done:

"I would guess that only 20% of the global financial institutions could be considered eligible at this time for the advanced internal ratings approach to economic capital for the proposed new Basle guidelines."

And Robert Statius-Muller of Greenwich Associates opines that, however effective current risk management techniques are, the investment banks are late to the party:

"Risk is inextricably entwined with the shareholder value [SV] concept. Few investment banks have truly grasped SV, although Bankers Trust and JP Morgan have been working on risk-adjusted capital models for years in pricing their deals. I'm astonished how long it has taken for the investment banking industry to adopt the concept of risk-adjusted capital; it took the BIS [Bank for International Settlements] guidelines to beat them into it!"

As mentioned above, even Goldman Sachs did not have in place in 1994 an aggregate market risk control system when it suffered substantial losses on its interest rate book.[31]

Getting the organizational structure right is widely seen as essential for overall risk management. Many of our sources cited the partnership structure – once again – as the ideal vehicle for risk management. The common interest of all partners in preserving their personal wealth can play the role of the cultural deterrent mentioned above by Amelia Fawcett in a stockholder-owned bank.

In this context, the historical tradition of Goldman Sachs in pairing a senior trader and investment banker as co-heads of the bank not only served to improve communication but also ensured that both views were expressed on risk-related issues. Whatever the corporate structure, however, best practice today requires a senior risk manager close to the top of the organization and responsible for managing aggregate risks.

What is the bottom line of these messages from professionals dealing with risk? Once again, there is almost total agreement on best practice. This would include: risk models fully stress-tested and managed by experienced professionals who can apply judgement in difficult circumstances; a culture which stresses values such as communication to identify possible fraud or human error; aggregate risk measurement across the organization, and a management structure which places a senior risk officer near the top of the management tree to manage the process.

Yet our conversations made it clear that the unexpected risk remains to bedevil the best of best practice. As Richard Ramsden of Goldman Sachs puts it:

> *"The biggest risks are those we don't know about! Today there's increasing concern about off-balance sheet commitments. And no one knows how some of these new products, say credit derivatives, will perform in a bear market."*

Dick Thornburgh of CSFB, who supervises most of the firm's risk functions, agrees that product risk is of concern:

> *"In every bull market, Wall Street develops new ways to meet customer needs, but customers don't always appreciate the downside. For example, in the 1990s people regarded the supercharged cash product as a money market fund with a guaranteed net asset value of $1.00 until rates spiked and they lost a lot of money. Today you have credit problems like Enron which lead to reputational risk. You have very sophisticated investors who bought products without thinking about the liquidity risk – a run on the bank."*

Göran Björling of SHB echoes this concern:

> *"The big risk is not market or counterpart in general but the complexity of products. Things like barrier options are so complex that the operations and control functions must be highly specialized."*

And the final word comes from the former JP Morgan banker Martin O'Neil:

> *"There'll always be a 100 year flood; the key is not to be more affected than your peers!"*

8
Cost Management

"It's a permanent challenge to keep costs as variable as possible. We haven't had a lot of success."

– Marcel Ospel, UBS

Managing costs is always difficult in a volatile, market-driven business. When the dominant cost item is the human capital which constitutes the guts of the business and the basis for essential client relationships, the challenge is formidable. And when the cost base is inflated further by heavy fixed investment in global infrastructure and product platforms, the winners are truly separated from the losers.

Investment banking is all of the above. I asked each of my interviewees the obvious questions: what management techniques and processes can address these cost issues? Is there any way of avoiding the savaging of the key human resource in a sustained down market such as that of 2001–02? And is a root and branch restructuring of the industry's vast and complex infrastructure realistic as a measure to bring costs into line with revenues?

Let's look first at some relevant statistics.

The compensation/revenue ratio is a key benchmark for many businesses, but in investment banking it is arguably the most widely-used operating guideline in a sector in which people costs can account for 60–70 per cent of the total. While it excludes the rising cost of stock options granted, the benchmark ratio of compensation costs/net revenue for most banks has not deviated significantly from 50 per cent in recent years, while the ratio of other expenses has fallen slightly. Figure 8.1 plots these ratios for the major US investment banks for the period 1998–2001.

Spending on technology is another major cost driver, accounting in recent years for an estimated average 14–15 per cent of total costs. Table 8.1 lists a consultant's estimate of spending for the year 2000; most global

Figure 8.1 Key cost ratios for US investment banks[1]

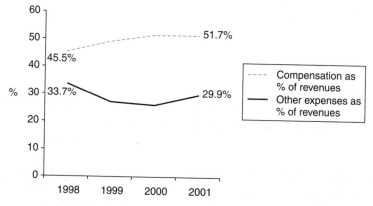

Note: 1. Average for eight banks.
Source: Fitch Ratings.

Table 8.1 Global investment bank IT spending patterns

Investment bank	IT spend 2000 ($m)	Total operating expenses 2000 ($m)	IT spend as a percentage of total operating expenses
Deutsche Bank	3200	10 988	29
Citigroup	3100	38 559	8
UBS	2700	26 203	10
JP Morgan Chase	2454	22 824	11
Crédit Suisse First Boston	2400	9 368	26
ABN Amro	2400	13 744	17
Merrill Lynch	2320	21 070	11
Morgan Stanley Dean Witter & Co	1556	17 936	9
Goldman Sachs	440	11 570	4

Source: Andersen, *Euromoney*.

Table 8.2 Evolution of US investment bank personnel costs and revenues, 1990–2001E ($ billion)

	1990	1995	2000	2001E	% increase, 1990–2000	% decrease, 2000–2001
Revenues	31.4	58.1	134.7	109.3	329	(19)
Headcount (000)						
Income-producing	73.7	103.5	160.8	136.9	118	(15)
All other	136.2	155.7	204.6	175.3	50	(14)

Sources: SIA (Securities Industry Association) and Bernstein.

investment banks would appear to have spent over $2 billion each. Even assuming the data is reasonably accurate and consistently calculated, however, there is no means of evaluating how much value was created.

Another means of tracking cost increments in a highly volatile business is to examine the relative evolution of headcount over the business cycle against revenues. Table 8.2 tracks this development for US investment banks over the period 1990 (a low point on the cycle) to 2001, another down year. Headcount has tracked revenue growth, but at a somewhat slower pace. In 2001, the drop in headcount was less drastic than the fall in revenues.

Applying costs to individual products is a more challenging task, but a recent study by McKinsey and JP Morgan Chase provides some useful estimates for major cost categories for three key products: US listed stocks, European cash equities, and derivatives.[32] Figure 8.2 summarizes this analysis.

Figure 8.2 Breakdown of global broker–dealer cost base, 1999–2000

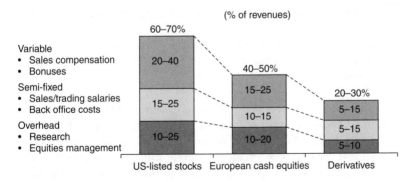

Source: McKinsey estimate based on sample of selected players.

Among other things, Figure 8.2 reveals the wide spread in overall cost margins across products and the substantial overall margin on derivatives – not surprising given the amount of cross-subsidization discussed in Chapter 3.

Our starting point is the common assumption that investment banking is a revenue-driven business. Volatility in that revenue stream is a fact of life. Management's challenge is to maximize their share of that revenue stream, hopefully by winning a top three to five position in each sector.

The primordial drive for revenues entails incremental costs. Building platforms for the European market, for example, required massive outlays for the US bulge group in the 1990s. New offices were opened across the world to achieve proximity to clients as well as to build global distribution. Costly trading platforms link the firm's dealing network with clients on a global scale. Global equity research departments to support sales and trading as well as investment banking have reached staffing levels of 600–700 professionals for the leaders.

Derivatives and other product specialists spotting a new product opportunity demand the front end and middle office systems to support and control that new initiative. And this front-office-led spending wave brings with it the need for human resource, facilities management, risk control and a host of other support functions.

So what are the management techniques used to manage this cost base with a view to maximizing long-term stockholder value? The question was particularly relevant in mid-2002, as the industry faced the possibility of a third successive year of flat or declining revenues after the bull market peak of 2000. And it is relevant for the industry's long-term future, whatever the length of the current revenue drought.

One of the many banks to acknowledge overspending during the boom years is Enskilda Securities. Its CEO Per-Anders Ovin admits that

> *"You have to be more careful in expanding when times are good. You can cut back but it causes lots of pain. We got a little carried away – we tried to do too many things at the same time."*

The first and most prevalent response of our interview sample is to maximize the proportion of variable costs. As indicated by Figure 8.2, these can be substantial. The partnership concept in which today's investment bank is rooted made the simple and logical assumption that variable compensation is the dominant portion of professional costs and that it could theoretically be zero in a bad year.

Amelia Fawcett of Morgan Stanley thus expresses a common view:

"Compensation cost is 50–60% of the total, depending on the firm, so the first solution is to pay less in a bad year. You say to your people: 'You can have a job but you are going to get paid 40% less than last year'."

This may be possible for an industry leader like Morgan Stanley, especially in a down year like 2002 when the job market is weak, but for a lesser player like HSBC it can be painful. We mentioned in Chapter 7 the departures provoked by cutting presumably variable bonus costs in line with the remuneration policy articulated earlier in the book by many of our interviewees. Whatever the merits of the opposing arguments, the result may cause analysts to query the assumption of variability in bonus costs.

Another limitation on slashing variable compensation is the eternal struggle to retain top people who can move easily to another job. Graham Clempson of Deutsche Bank explains:

"Deutsche Bank will skew the compensation to protect the best people and encourage a sense of ownership, a culture of teamwork when conditions are bad."

And then there is the variable compensation paid to salesmen – a substantial portion of the variable element shown in Figure 8.2. Such compensation will inevitably drop with volume, but a case can also be made for increasing such compensation rates paid to client-facing staff in order to stimulate volume in a down year.

It is technology spend, however, which is the biggest barrier to the ideal of maximizing variable costs. Whereas in commercial banking the concept of outsourcing non-strategic functions such as transaction processing, supply management and human resource administration is gathering pace, in investment banking this practice has met with strong resistance. A typical response is that of SHB's Göran Björling:

"We try to keep processing in-house to maintain quality."

Speaking of the long-standing negotiations to collaborate on joint cost-saving projects like straight-through processing (STP), Richard Ramsden concludes:

"Investment banks have a big problem in co-operating with each other to share facilities. Management needs to feel comfortable that they control

data processing to meet regulatory standards. And they are reluctant to outsource economies of scale."

Two major outsourcing initiatives, however, have been taken during the past decade by major investment banks in partnership with leading processing and consulting firms. The former JP Morgan and Swiss Bank Corporation (now UBS) each targeted not only ongoing cost savings but also shifting fixed costs off their P & L to be replaced by variable costs based on per-unit charges. For example, Morgan's Pinnacle Alliance announced in 1996 aimed at maximizing variable costs, reducing overall expenses on the relevant cost base by 15 per cent, and accessing the best specialist expertise.

On the basis of our interviews with these banks, neither project seems to have been a sparkling success. UBS' Chairman Marcel Ospel, who headed Swiss Bank Corporation when the alliance with Perot Systems was agreed, summarizes the current position:

"It's a permanent challenge to keep costs as variable as possible; we haven't had a lot of success. As for the Perot alliance, we seriously overestimated the potential of the partnership."

Somewhat the same tone is struck by Mark Garvin at JP Morgan:

"We're reviewing the Pinnacle Alliance [with three technology partners]. We're not dogmatic about outsourcing but will look at the numbers. A virtue of outsourcing is transparency; you know the full cost of what you're paying. The basic principle is to distinguish between core and non-core activities: core is proprietary, relating to one's one own competitive advantage and business-aligned, and that's kept in-house. But, for example, running a data centre or PC help desk is generic."

Whatever the reasons behind this muted evaluation several years after the launch, the outside observer has to conclude that, if two well-managed and experienced global banks are not enthused about major outsourcing initiatives, the prospects for swapping fixed for variable costs in the middle and back offices are not brilliant.

A second widely-used benchmark is the ratio of compensation to net revenues as a key management tool to limit the growth of headcount and compensation cost not matched by corresponding revenue generation. As indicated above in Figure 8.1, the magic figure is 50 per cent, which has been achieved by most of the leading firms in recent years.

The role model for this cost discipline is Lehman Brothers, whose remarkable development since 1994 is widely attributed at least in part to such rigour. Jeremy Isaacs, Lehman's CEO-Europe and Asia summarizes the firm's philosophy:

> *"Understanding the revenue opportunity, appreciation of the total costs associated with the revenue stream and disciplined management of these costs lie at the very heart of the Lehman strategy. Managing the cost base is not a strategy just for difficult market conditions – it's the lifeblood of creating shareholder value for any organisation."*

One of Lehman's many admirers is Eileen Fahey of the Fitch rating agency:

> *"Lehman controls costs extremely well. After the 1994 spin-off, they introduced a mantra of 'grow revenues but within a cost and risk return framework'. They have abided by their parameters and were the only major US firm able to add people in 2002, as well as outperformed their peers. The cost base is a major driver of their strategy."*

We profile Lehman Brothers in Chapter 10 in part because of the success of this discipline.

Another advocate of Lehman's discipline is Sir Win Bischoff of Citigroup:

> *"Starting with the kind of organization you want to be, with its implications for margins and ROE, you can fix the cost relationships on a consistent basis. Thus Fuld of Lehman has set a 50% comp/revenue goal and stuck to it. You make it known throughout the organization. People know that revenue drives the business, but they also know what costs are acceptable."*

A third strategy is to cull staff regularly rather than be forced into periodic crash lay-offs when revenues collapse. The role model for this strategy is Goldman Sachs, who has dropped perhaps 3–5 per cent of its total staff among the low performers every year almost regardless of market conditions.

McKinsey's Mark Williams applauds the strategy:

> *"Best practice is to cut costs fast in a way that doesn't disturb your client franchise and your recruiting effort. Rescinding recruiting offers or firing relationship managers can be very damaging. Good cost management*

requires an external, not just an internal focus. In any case, losing the bottom 10–15% of staff should be a regular process."

Robert Colthorpe of Société Générale also agrees:

"You need to cut costs quickly, with integrity and as transparently as possible. It's part of a continuous process. There needs to be constant communication as to why it's being done, and you need to emote with people whether they stay or not. It's the test of strong leadership."

William Connelly of ING Barings also espouses the Goldman Sachs approach:

"You have to be ruthless in pruning poor performers. The bottom 5% has to leave every year to upgrade the quality of execution. There also needs to be more differentiation in pay: good corporate finance professionals should get top quartile pay, while the 'safe pair of hands' should get fourth quartile."

A final strategy is to take a top-down review of all the firm's businesses – essentially a strategic rethink – with a view to exiting the loss or low-profit segments. While this does not exclude also pursuing the policies described above, it is particularly relevant in a sustained down market such as the current one.

Goldman Sachs' Peter Weinberg describes the process:

"It's a top-down process. We look at the overall industry, product by product, and evaluate where the world will be in five years time. Then we look at the role Goldman could potentially play, which doesn't necessarily mean being number one in everything. Next, we examine the people implications – their cost and contribution – to make sure we have the appropriate focus and scale. The result is a logical framework within which to make decisions."

Overshadowing all of these cost strategies is the sizeable overhang of the infrastructure and technology cost base. In the interview series I heard a number of friends speak of the need to carry out a root and branch review of the overall back office and support functions with a view to taking a massive slice out of the cost base.

Deutsche Bank in particular is under pressure from both investors and top management anxious to boost its stock price. Graham Clempson outlines the problem:

> *"The cost reduction issue is one of enormous complexity. With legacy and other systems, everyone is working with an increasingly complex interaction. You need to take a root and branch approach to the model – not just incremental change. More technology leads to more complexity. We are asking ourselves questions like 'Do you need multiple dealing units; what can we centralize?' You can imagine the impact on the Deutsche Bank stock price from taking out $2 billion of costs."*

Another continental banker bemoans the heavy cost of a traditional universal bank, where considerable duplication of effort and over staffing is a burden.

The burden of general overhead is a particular annoyance to hard-pressed investment bankers. ING's William Connelly believes:

> *"You must have accountability for indirect costs like human resources and compliance."*

His concern is echoed by Nicholas Coulson of NM Rothschild:

> *"You have to keep a sharp eye on the ratio between revenue-generators and support staff. Staff functions like HR can mushroom as the firm grows. At NM Rothschild there are no bankers who do nothing but manage."*

Oliver, Wyman & Co. consultant Simon Harris describes the process by which investment banks have created both complexity and high cost in their effort to build revenues:

> *"Banks have spent a fortune on technology both to 'run the bank' and to 'change the bank'. For 'change the bank', someone needs to offer the latest product, so you construct or upgrade a system, especially in a bull market. One bolts something on to an existing platform and builds up a patchwork of systems. There are always new ideas from the revenue producers with the middle office struggling to catch up with the front office. It's not a legacy problem as in commercial banking, but a patch-work of proprietary systems with modern technology – it's five, not twenty five years old."*

Those charged with the task of addressing the infrastructure cost issue have a particularly difficult assignment.

Chief Information Officer for the Corporate and Investment Bank at Deutsche Bank, Mitchel Lenson, explains the background and his strategy in a recent *Euromoney* article:

> "*Traditionally at Deutsche Bank time-to-market was the most important thing for us. The focus was not on cost but on becoming a bulge bracket firm ... our focus today has more of a balance between costs and revenue ... the legacy has created this support and maintenance need in order to run the bank. This is a large part of what we do, and the reality is we have to re-engineer off those existing systems. The change-the-bank side is discretionary and set by management ... we want to push down our run-the-bank number 5% year on year as a minimum. We keep the 'change-the-bank' part as flat as possible. ... when you've got a massive legacy system it takes time to wind down and it isn't going to happen overnight.*"[33]

Consultant Jon Robertson of Accenture offers a more pungent and pessimistic view in the same article:

> "*Running their own processing shops is always the last bastion of arrogance, but banks have so much money they can afford to get away with it. If you look at any other industry that is as mature as investment banking, they have already taken up completely different models.*"[34]

Another consultant, Svilen Ivanov of The Boston Consulting Group, levels a broadside at cost management in the sector:

> "*The problem is that they don't have a holistic view of cost. They can manage the front office capacity by hiring and firing, but they keep building back office costs. Rather than outsource or fundamentally rethink the operational side, they simply cut a percentage of support costs.*"

Whether driven by in-house resistance to change, the dominance of revenue-generators demanding their proprietary systems, or top management unable to impose cost discipline, it is hard to be optimistic over the prospects for such a root and branch transformation of investment banking infrastructure. The mixed results from the two major outsourcing initiatives described above are not a positive augury for the future. For years investment bank managements have enthused over the prospects for combining forces on projects such as straight-through processing (STP) to take a massive bite out of the cost base, but such projects remain on the drawing board.

Are major staff reductions thus inevitable in a major downturn? Barring an unlikely revolution in managing infrastructure costs, and given the other limitations described above, the answer of most of our sources is a resounding 'yes'.

Donald Moore of Morgan Stanley summarizes his views:

> *"You start by going for the easy wins; they're easy to find as there is much less focus on expenses in the good years. After the easy wins, you ask yourself 'How can we reconfigure the business?' You lead with your infrastructure costs, including your IT platform, but at the end of the day you've got to cut people, since they generate the costs."*

Chairman Marcel Ospel of UBS agrees:

> *"If margins had collapsed, it would be easier, but when volume collapses you can't do much about compensation, so you have to reduce staff – shrink the business."*

Assaad Razzouk, formerly deputy head of global corporate finance at Nomura International, takes a straightforward view of the cost issue:

> *"Most successful investment banks have done well because they've followed best practice benchmarking – specifically the comp/net revenues formula. The good ones are all in the same band. When revenues drop, costs have to as well, so some people have to go."*

Is such volatility in the human resource base a major issue? Does one destroy a firm's culture and damage client relationships by cutting client-facing professionals?

Nick O'Donohoe of JP Morgan Chase offers a philosophical view:

> *"70 per cent of costs are people; to cut costs you have to get rid of some people. The rest is a rounding error. Cutting back on first-class travel simply infuriates people. It's easy to do nothing in good times, but I'd argue that you should cut back 10% every year to cull out the weak performers."*

"Your job security is your clients, skills and the profit you generate. The culture has changed. There is no unique culture. Everyone is doing the same thing with the same kind of people."

Managing the cost base raises another issue of the relationship between costs and revenues. Termed 'operational leverage', 'scalability' or 'right sizing', it essentially refers to a bank's ability over time to match its cost base to its long-term revenue-generating potential.

The assumption of firms winning market share in their chosen segments is that they will benefit from positive operational leverage – in effect, increasing both revenue and margins at the expense of those drained of revenue who will be encouraged to exit the segment. Also termed the 'high-cost, high-revenue model', it underpins the business strategy of the global bulge bracket group. During the 2001–02 downturn of the equity and M & A markets, it seems to have been borne out in practice, as the market share of the leaders has generally increased.

The challenge for other firms is either to reduce their cost base or to find other businesses to grow. This is particularly true for the mid-sized European banks refocusing on their home market strengths.

Table 8.3 provides a rough estimate of the challenge facing both the global and mid-sized banks. Using the cost per employee as a benchmark and assuming rough comparability of data, it would appear that the global firms have proportionately a much higher cost base than most of their smaller European competitors.

Assuming some of the global firms with a higher cost base must eventually retrench, the issue for them is whether they can 'right size' the

Table 8.3 Estimated 2000 cost per head of selected investment banks (in US $000 annualized)

Deutsche (GCI)	676
UBS	632
Crédit Suisse/DLJ pro forma	563
Goldman Sachs (Group)	533
Commerzbank	523
Lehman	485
Dresdner	387
Société Générale (CIB)	327
ABN Amro	301

Source: Lehman Brothers.

business around a new revenue model to achieve their profitability goals. By the same token, the challenge for the mid-sized banks is also whether they can adjust their cost configuration so as to generate profits from the likely smaller revenue base. This could actually require increasing costs by investing in competitive delivery systems and products, or it might simply require shedding costs not relevant to the new strategy.

We address this issue in the final chapter of the book.

One of the most fascinating challenges is the cost of research. The bull market of the 1990s has in effect enlisted – or hijacked, depending on your point of view – the muscle of investment banks' research arms to support the investment bankers' quest for mandates. The result has been a ballooning of research staffs to levels of 600–700 professionals for the global banks. At perhaps $1 million all-in cost per professional, that constitutes a hefty expense which would appear fixed as long as a global research effort is required.

While the headlines in mid-2002 have focused on the issue of transparency and integrity of advice, lurking behind this issue is the more fundamental one of who will pay for this research bill. Traditionally borne by the equity sales and trading function which markets their research to clients, over the 1990s an increasing portion – say 40–50 per cent – has been carried by the investment banking business.

For banks suffering from a drought in investment banking mandates and perhaps weak in secondary trading volume as well, the burden of research costs is a heavy one. Nick O'Donohoe of JP Morgan Chase explains the dilemma:

"Our challenge is to build our equity business. We're number eight in the league tables. We have limited retail distribution, so we can't spread our equity research costs over retail distribution as can Citigroup and Merrill. In that sense we're sub-scale. How do we justify research when Goldman Sachs has the same cost base but much higher equities revenues?"

Svilen Ivanov of The Boston Consulting Group agrees that this is a widespread concern:

"How do you get paid for research if you have a weak investment banking function? It's a real problem for some second-tier players, who are the ones who will really get hurt!"

Marcel Ospel of UBS acknowledges:

"Research will go through a paradigm change."

In sum, a sustained period of overcapacity and revenue drought is likely to generate ongoing staff reductions. Even the most disciplined firms like Goldman Sachs and Lehman, with staff costs between 60–70 per cent of the total, must eventually cut back. After the 1998 market collapse, following the Russian crisis, the bulge group firmly maintained that they had learned the lesson of earlier cutbacks in 1994. At that time those firms like CSFB who cut back only lost market share and had to rehire people as the market quickly picked up.

In 2002, however, we heard no mention of 1994 or 1998. Management acknowledged that this revenue drought was a totally different animal from its predecessors.

If significant cuts in staffing are necessary, what will separate the winners from the losers? We suspect that it will be the same disciplined managers who make regular culls rather than periodic, reactive cutbacks; who use the comp/revenue ratio as an ongoing control benchmark, and who periodically review their strategic configuration to cull the low-profit businesses. And perhaps who also apply the same discipline to their infrastructure costs!

9
Growing by Mergers and Acquisitions

"The phrase 'investment bank merger' is an oxymoron!"
– Richard Boath, Barclays Capital

Only three years ago, this chapter would probably not have been written. The leaders in today's investment banking model were former partnerships which had grown by and large organically, eschewing the cultural dilution and conflict which accompanied a major merger or acquisition. Buying into another 'people' business risked not only losing key professionals but also paying a substantial premium over book value for these same people.

In the 1980s and early 1990s, the track record of acquiring or merging investment banks was patchy at best. Outsiders in particular lost millions on mergers by buying into the business without being able to make a substantive contribution or understanding its dynamics. American Express' purchase of Lehman, General Electric's buying into Kidder Peabody, and the wholesale destruction of UK merchant banks and brokers by their domestic and foreign acquirers after Big Bang in the UK, led many to conclude that acquiring an investment bank was a thoroughly bad idea.

Norman Bernard of First Consulting articulates the pessimist's view:

"There's not much success, but lots of destruction, in investment bank mergers. Do merged banks actually achieve real scale advantage or simply make their business more complex? Investment bankers aren't very good at managing complexity. Most investment bankers are specialists, with client relationships which often go back decades. Mergers simply lump more of them together, and they all continue to do the same thing as before the merger. It's very hard to get them to change!"

How the world has changed! In 2002 five of the eight global leaders are banks which have entered the magic circle largely via the merger route, bringing with them a powerful balance sheet as well as a competitive array of people and products.

Whether or not the merger trend at the top continues, growth by acquisitions is an established strategic alternative, perhaps even the preferred route for the future as the titans battle for market share. It poses a number of questions. Why incur the merger risks which historically have deterred acquirers in this business? How have these mergers worked in practice? And, most important of all, what lessons can be drawn from merger experience in investment banking?

In the context of this last question, I am particularly interested in the comparison with merger experience in the commercial or universal banking sector which was analysed in an earlier book.[35]

The consensus of our interview sample was clear: market share in desirable segments is the dominant objective of a merger strategy. Maureen Erasmus of Lehman Brothers puts it succinctly:

"The goal of a merger is to win a step change in market position. It needs to be really revenue-transforming to be worthwhile. Size itself is not important. The market looks for constant revenue growth, cost management and focused execution. If the gap is filled by an acquisition, the market will reward you."

The problem, of course, is actually measuring the increment to market share. Combining the two merging firms on a pro forma basis may or may not be appropriate, as clients may not continue to provide the merged firm with the same combined business volume. And other variables may intervene to influence the outcome.

Thus one of the most controversial acquisitions in recent years, that of DLJ by CSFB in 2000, provides mixed evidence in terms of the metric of market share. On the one hand, Dick Thornburgh of CSFB points out that market share improved in high yield, global equity, prime brokerage and mortgage-backed securities. In addition:

"We got there quicker, along with improved operating leverage, as front office numbers increased 48% and the back office only 7%."

On the other hand, pessimists note that the combined market share of the firm following the merger has declined in several key businesses. Figure 9.1 tracks this erosion for the key sector of US IPOs (Initial

Figure 9.1 Post-merger loss of market share by CSFB/DLJ in US IPOs

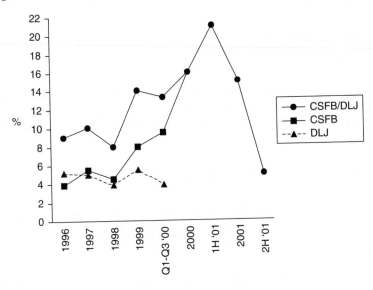

Sources: SDC, Bloomberg, Bernstein Research.

Public Offerings), which can at least in part be attributed to the collapse in CSFB's specialty of technology offerings.

In addition, the massive departure of DLJ professionals is widely seen as a negative for the group. While several DLJ professionals obtained key executive positions in the merged bank, observers regard the acquisition as an expensive one in terms of talent retained.

What are the lessons of a successful merger process? In a people business where duplication of jobs is likely to be widespread, how does one retain the professionals and capabilities one wants without ending up with a bloated cost base and an unhappy team?

One lesson with which all of our interviewees concur is the need for strong direction from one – presumably the larger – partner. For Marcel Ospel of UBS, who is highly regarded for his success as a serial acquirer, the lessons have not changed over the years:[37]

> *"There's no change in the lessons: speed is important, and there's no such thing as a merger of equals. The clients, shareholders and staff want results!"*

Dick Thornburgh agrees with a firm and speedy timetable for the array of acquisitions made by CSFB:

> *"Decide quickly on the leaders and limit compromises. Make tough decisions and get on with it."*

BNP Paribas' CEO Michel Pebereau receives the ultimate accolade from Patrick Soulard at rival Société Générale. In Soulard's view, the success of the difficult BNP Paribas merger is attributable largely to the fact that:

> *"Pebereau was the only pilot on board."*

Sir Win Bischoff of Citigroup, whose experience covers both the acquisitions he managed as head of Schroders as well as the subsequent purchase of Schroders by Citigroup, agrees:

> *"The key is to recognize that one group of people is in charge – that this is an acquisition, not a merger of equals. The Citi people wanted to retain some aspects of the Schroders culture, but it is clear that the old Travelers team is in charge. Successful mergers include SBC/UBS and perhaps – somewhat less so – JP Morgan Chase. The former may have lost of lot of old UBS people, and the process may be cruel and unfair, but the alternative is a 'we and they' culture."*

Ron Carlson, who has played a major role in the integration process of Merrill Lynch's multiple acquisitions in Europe, sets out several lessons of experience:

> *"First, people are the most important factor in a merger. You need to set the tone at the top, and it cascades down. Second, there's no cookie cutter approach; each integration situation is different. Thirdly, integrating with pace is better than leaving the acquisition alone. Any existing problems won't go away. If you're up front, you have conflict but can then move on. Finally, losing people isn't the only factor in a dynamic investment banking market. In the case of several regional brokers we acquired, we did experience some turnover. People have different aspirations, and they move on. But we've been able to replace them and successfully retool the business."*

Richard Boath of Barclays Capital takes a pragmatic view of the acquisition process:

> *"The phrase 'investment bank merger' is an oxymoron. What works is a growth strategy with acquisitions as a core part of the strategy. Look at Citigroup. Sandy Weill bought a series of businesses and essentially said: 'I'm in charge, I'm buying your business. This is what we will be doing; are you part of the team; if not, good-bye.' Acquisitions like that do work."*

How fast should one integrate? The issue has been a painful one for several European acquirers. As described in *Bank Mergers*, Deutsche Bank bought the British merchant bank Morgan Grenfell in 1990 and only began to integrate it several years later on the assumption that to move faster would be to destroy its unique culture.[36] In a similar fashion, ABN Amro acquired strong brokerages in the UK (Hoare Govett) and Scandinavia (A. Berg) and left them essentially alone for the same reason.

In the case of Deutsche Bank, management in retrospect felt it should have integrated much sooner and did so in the purchase of Bankers Trust. With regard to ABN Amro's strategy, most of Berg's top management team left years later when the parent began to integrate its investment banking function. Several of our Scandinavian sources were highly critical of the Dutch bank's handling of the situation. As one puts it:

> *"Why did ABN Amro buy them in the first place? Berg was the most fiercely independent of all the investment banks. They don't tolerate interference from outside."*

There are clearly no easy answers on this central issue of timing and flexibility of integration. In its acquisition of Crédit Commercial de France, HSBC aims to tread with sensitivity. Investment banking head Stephen Green, who represents HSBC on CCF's board, explains:

> *"HSBC has paid lots of attention to continuity and maintaining culture – not marching in with hob-nailed boots. It's important to maintain self-respect and to nurture rather than destroy. A consultant might say that there could be more rationalization and that more could be cut, but HSBC tries to maintain motivation. And there's a difference between buying a successful business like CCF and a problem one."*

Hans Morris at Citigroup, who has played a role in several of the group's investment banking mergers, distinguishes between essential change and the scope for flexibility:

> "At Citigroup and Travelers, there's an absolute way of doing mergers. We have a high degree of confidence in our ability to execute – almost a play-book on how to do it. There are some things that are always on the check list, like achieving cost objectives; in every merger someone 'owns' this objective and is designated as 'having the whistle' to make the decisions quickly. Further, the people who do the diligence before the deal own the problems after the deal. But there's no one single model. Some things have to be dealt with immediately; in other cases the model can evolve. We're always listening, and in many cases, adjusting. It would have been a mistake to have moved quickly on the structuring of the Corporate and Investment Bank."

Robert Statius-Muller of Greenwich Associates also argues for flexibility:

> "The magic is to find the right balance between control/integration and continued independence/freedom. You need to be focused to get the full benefit of the merger. But investment banks are sufficiently different, with a degree of integration not true of other businesses. The success stories like Schroders Salomon Smith Barney/Citibank have an ongoing degree of separation, whereas ABN Amro, trying to integrate its regional brokers, squeezed out the unique qualities of its investment bankers, like Berg, where the rainmakers have left."

Per-Anders Ovin, head of Enskilda Securities and formerly a senior executive at Berg, offers a fascinating perspective. Enskilda acquired the Norwegian brokerage Orkla and theoretically could face the same problems as ABN Amro with Berg:

> "Managing mergers is extremely difficult. The Orkla merger is OK. We've succeeded by being relaxed, by not pushing it too fast. A lot depends on how integrated it is. Does it need to be integrated? The goal is to create common values so you're not too people-dependent. ABN Amro believed in integration at any price. You knew they couldn't do it because they had different values. We said to ourselves: 'What does ABN offer us?' Enskilda and Orkla are complementary; each offers a benefit to the other."

The downside risk of investment banking mergers, of course, is the loss of key people as well as the premium over book value paid to buy their business. Goldman Sachs' Richard Ramsden describes the pitfalls:

> *"There are two issues. First, what are you buying? As the CSFB/DLJ situation shows, everyone in the target company becomes a free agent, and you have to pay again to keep them. And secondly, the combined market share is up for grabs. A client like Fidelity wants to maintain a broad array of suppliers and won't simply give the same amount of business to the combined firm."*

Martin Smith, who built DLJ's European franchise, agrees:

> *"Buying an investment bank can be simply an option to offer people a job, because the good ones will have plenty of offers from the competition."*

In this context, retention payments to ensure that key individuals remain in the job for a minimum period of time have become an integral part of the compensation package.

Our interviewees agree that the best investment bank merger is a complementary one with minimum overlap. Thus Morgan Stanley's acquisition of Dean Witter's retail franchise wins widespread plaudits. The turmoil of an overlapping merger in the business evokes a colourful comment from Nicholas Coulson of NM Rothschild:

> *"Where there's duplication, people are fighting for their lives. Investment bankers are some of the meanest street fighters in the world. If you put them in charge of a merger you get ethnic cleansing."*

A friend at Société Générale in Paris notes with regret his bank's experience with acquiring investment banks and brokers:

> *"We've been a bad buyer in investment banking, partly because we bought businesses to learn them, partly because we paid top dollar for cyclical businesses, then paid high bonuses, and ended up writing off goodwill!"*

A friend at ING Barings agrees that buying an investment bank to learn the business is not the ideal strategy:

> *"ING sort of stumbled into corporate finance; they bought Barings for its emerging market business and fund management. They didn't understand the corporate finance side and left us on our own for a while."*

For Walter Gubert of JP Morgan, the answer to the integration dilemma is to build common cultural values:

> "What are the lessons of merger integration? Don't underestimate the cultural issues – they kill most investment banking mergers. Management is distracted, and with few exceptions (such as JP Morgan), lose market share in the year after the merger. How do you deal with these issues? First you make decisions early on. It's not easy. You create clarity as soon as possible. Second, we went on a global road show internally to describe how we do business: what are our values?, how do we manage credit?, what is the client management function?, etc. Speed and clarity: if you do it right, you can manage the cultural divisions. It's a new firm – not the old ways of doing things. You spend a month looking at each business and issue and take the best of each."

His colleague Mark Garvin adds some lessons from his role in managing four acquisitions made in Europe by the former Chemical Bank:

> "It's critical to have a clear vision underpinned by strong execution. We typically look at a two-year time frame. The first year is devoted to implementation, while the second year is about optimisation. It's very high energy – everyone is engaged. The merger process is a catalyst for forging new management teams. We tell people that the demons are outside, not inside the firm, and to focus their energy on clients."

A friend at Citigroup, describing the successful blending of commercial and investment bankers in the group, points out:

> "There was a high degree of cynicism about the marriage of Salomon and Citi. But we've done well. When you put two gorillas in a cage, there has to be mutual respect for each other's contribution. And that mutual respect exists."

Who are seen as the successful investment banking mergers and the leaders of that merger process?

Top of the list for our interview sample comes Citigroup. A typical comment comes from a veteran British banker:

> "Schroder Salomon Smith Barney is a great success story. People joke that in the past, an hour meeting with the old Schroder gave you an hour of

independent advice; now you get ten minutes of that advice and 50 minutes of hard sell on balance sheet products. The dialogue has changed! But the result is a lot more business and profits, and everybody seems happy. Sandy Weill seems to walk on water."

Former JP Morgan investment banker Martin O'Neil echoes that view:

"The real winner is Sandy Weill! Imagine buying Smith Barney, merging it into Salomon Brothers, closing down Sollie's prop trading business, and then buying Citibank, followed by Schroders. If there is a reincarnation, its successor is Citibank! The universal banking model has legitimized itself!"

Another frequently mentioned successful merger practitioner is the former Swiss Bank Corporation management now running UBS. As Mark Williams of McKinsey puts it:

"The old SBC has done it well repeatedly – first O'Connor, where they handed over the keys, second SG Warburg, a fantastic equity house, and lastly UBS, brutal but fast."

Finally, as indicated above, complementary mergers and acquisitions win high praise. In addition to Morgan Stanley's acquisition of Dean Witter to provide both diversification as well as placing power, our sources speak highly of Merrill Lynch's purchase of Smith New Court in London to provide European research and trading strength.

So what lessons can the outsider draw from this evidence? First, merger integration is much more challenging than the process for commercial banks described in *Bank Mergers*. There is a multiple in the number of key revenue-generators who can easily walk out the door if not happy with their deal. Serious economies can only be obtained at the cost of significant bloodshed at the client-facing end rather than the back office, whereas substantial economies in retail and commercial banking can be obtained by slashing relatively low-level staff and branch facilities.

Second, bringing people together in a mutually beneficial environment is a critical factor in the high performance investment banking world. Whether it be mutual self-interest and respect as in the case of Citigroup, the new common cultural values of JP Morgan Chase, or the synergies of Orkla and Enskilda Securities, the key professionals must feel that they obtain some value from the merger. Otherwise, as is so often the case in bringing commercial and investment bankers together under one tent, divorce seems the best solution. A recent example of the latter is the decision by Fleet Boston in the US to put up for sale its Robertson Stephens investment banking unit.

Thirdly, as Ron Carlson points out, all deals are different, and the successful acquirer needs to be attuned to these differences and able to inject some flexibility into the merger strategy. Whether or not ABN Amro can legitimately be accused of rigidity in their approach to Berg and other regional brokers is beyond the scope of this book, but the example of Citibank shows how the rule book can be rescripted if necessary.

Finally, the role of strong leadership – as always in a dynamic and performance-oriented business – is an essential ingredient for a successful merger. Having a Sandy Weill, Marcel Ospel or Michel Pebereau driving the process seems to have made the difference in so many cases. And, as we found in the commercial banking world, such leaders and their teams become sufficiently expert at the merger process to be able to repeat it again and again.

10
Case Studies in Success

"There's always a place for a leader, but none for a number seven."

— Lars Bertmar, Carnegie

"A team environment, and one with high expectations."

— Peter Weinberg, Goldman Sachs

An important dimension of the interview process was a straw poll designed to identify one or more leaders among the major investment banks which we could analyse in more detail in this chapter. Each of the investment bankers interviewed was thus asked 'Who is your most respected overall competitor?'

I make no claims for the intellectual rigour and statistical validity of this ranking. Some participants felt they could not cite specific names; others offered two. For mid-sized banks I attempted to gain their views on the global competitors in their market as well as local rivals. Perhaps more important than the actual ranking are the reasons given for the selection, and in the following profiles I list briefly most of the relevant comments made on specific candidates. It is these comments, proffered spontaneously by professionals who must compete in the global market-place, which I find most interesting in these profiles.

I also acknowledge that this is only a snapshot taken at a single moment in the evolution of an incredibly fast-moving business where perceptions of leadership change daily. As many participants pointed out, yesterday's also-ran can vault up the rankings in a very short period of time – and vice versa! And while I did not specify that the selection had to be made from the global bulge group, it is understandable in view of the global scope of our survey that few choices fell outside it.

On balance, I feel the sampling has some value if only as an indication of critical success factors, and I profile in this chapter the three most frequently-mentioned banks. Our profiles address three topics: what is the business profile and strategy; what do competitors respect in their business as well as operational models, and what challenges do the banks – and our interviewees – feel they must address to retain their leadership position?

The three most frequently-mentioned major firms and the number of votes accumulated are:

- Goldman Sachs – 21
- Citigroup – 14
- Morgan Stanley – 11

The validity of this sample is, in our view, considerably enhanced by the yawning gap between these three and all others. No other investment bank accumulated more than three votes as the 'most respected overall competitor'. Interestingly enough, many of those voting selected both Goldman and Morgan Stanley as two essentially equivalent role models in their own minds.

In addition, in our interview process it was clear that a number of firms outside the global bulge group also commanded the respect of our interview sample. We have thus added four banks whose business strategy and operating model seem to us to provide a broader range of excellence than one limited to the global bulge group:

- **Lehman Brothers** – its diversification strategy and cost discipline since flotation in 1994 have commanded the respect of many of our friends.
- **Cazenove** – the last of the pre-Big Bang UK brokers to have retained its independence, Cazenove remains a leader in its chosen specialities of company broker and financial advisor.
- **Macquarie Bank** – a leading investment bank in its Australian home market as well as a strong competitor on a global scale in cross-border project finance and tax-based leasing.
- **Carnegie Group** – one of the rare independent regional investment banks, it has maintained its leadership in the highly competitive Scandinavian market.

We profile first the three winners from our straw poll.

Goldman Sachs: a universally-admired operational model supports leadership in high-margin businesses

Goldman Sachs wins universal accolades across the entire investment banking spectrum for its operational model, which in turn supports its sustained leadership in the businesses of global M & A and equity issuance.

Goldman moved early in the 1990s to build almost from scratch its global capability in the targeted segments of M & A and equities. Heavy investment in Europe and other markets has generated not only a number one or two league table position since 1994 in these high-margin, strategic businesses but also the relatively high ROEs associated with them. Thus reported return on tangible shareholder's equity reached 28.9 per cent in the boom year of 2000, declining to a relatively high 17.8 per cent in 2001.

The contribution from non-US sources at an estimated 40 per cent is one of the highest of any of the bulge group. M & A and equities comprise a relatively elevated 38 per cent of global capital market revenues.

A distinguishing feature of the Goldman business model is focus on relatively profitable segments as well as those which are likely to generate captive clients. Thus in addition to the M & A and equities products which entail close working relationships with client CEOs, Goldman has captured brokerage business by its prime brokerage function and acquisition of US specialist market makers; invested heavily in merchant banking or private equity investments, and built market share in high-yield debt. Focus on the TMT sector in the late 1990s led to a major boost in technology-driven profits through 2000.

Sustaining this highly successful business strategy is an operating model which is the envy of peers from all corners of the investment banking world. Our conclusion from the interview series is that there is one ideal operating model across the business, and it is called Goldman Sachs!

Driven by Goldman's partnership ethos which has been sustained since its flotation in 1999, the model's key features are a 'one-bank' culture, common profit-sharing pool, single-minded focus on client service, and an intense, disciplined work ethic – all sustained by a long-standing list of 14 business principles or values which, unlike the case of most peers, is actually executed in practice. The list is attached as Appendix 2 at the end of this book not only because it an almost unique example of corporate values actually reflected in behaviour but also because of the number of banks which aspire to the same values.

While the firm is now a public company, perhaps half of its equity is held by present or past Goldman professionals, many of whom rely on that investment for a major portion of their net worth. This arguably tends to support management's efforts to create long-term shareholder value rather than short-term profits. Respect for this model and the results it generates is reflected in the unsolicited comments from our interview survey, which are listed below by source:

"the tennis game against Goldman starts with the score 30-love against you!" – ING Barings

"the firm can move 180 degrees overnight" – Lehman Brothers

"people want to work there" – JP Morgan Chase

"formidably well-managed" – HSBC

"their discipline earns them the name of 'the Moonies'" – Merrill Lynch

"they attract the cream of the crop of intense, high IQ people" – JP Morgan

"they pick the profitable bits" – Oliver Wyman

"stupendous client focus" – McKinsey & Co.

"the co-CEO concept has worked well" – Citigroup

"they compete like bull terriers in their client coverage model" – Lehman Brothers

To summarize the outcome, we quote Goldman's Peter Weinberg once again:

"Goldman Sachs has a tough, unforgiving culture, but we work together as a team: a team environment, and one with high expectations."

The downside of the operating model, as indicated by Weinberg, is its over-powering intensity and the time and effort needed to build consensus. The following quotes from our interviews illustrate the other side of the coin:

"they take ages to make up their minds" – JP Morgan

"no one 'retires'; they all get killed!" – Sanford Bernstein

"cracks are starting to appear in the model" – Deutsche Bank

"can they retain their human capital?" – Harvard Business School

The challenges facing the firm are quite clear. First, can it deflect the challenge posed by Citigroup and others with a much larger balance sheet as well as global capabilities? Weinberg articulates the firm's view:

> *"The commercial banks have tried hard to use their balance sheets as levers to win advisory business. In an economic environment where the provision of credit is critical, some would have expected lenders with advisory expectations to have done better in market share terms than they have. The proof that balance sheet size alone will win out simply isn't there. Our view is that the really critical issue is having an effective global foot print and the people who give us the ability to conduct the highest value business with clients who shape the future."*

The second challenge is to retain as much as possible of the old partnership operating model and culture. Part of the challenge is that posed by the firm's size, with over 20,000 in staff: in its 2001 Annual Report management articulates the problem as follows:

> *"Can we continue to manage growth by adapting our culture to the demands of a large and increasingly complex global company?"*

Weinberg acknowledges the problem:

> *"The benefits of the type of collaboration that a partnership culture encourages are considerable and should not be underestimated. While it is obvious that the firm is evolving, there is no doubt in my mind that people here recognise the benefits of our way of working."*

In Chapters 11 and 12 we provide our interviewees' and our own views on these and other issues.

Citigroup: globality, balance sheet power and product capabilities create a new contender for leadership

Through an astute acquisition and integration strategy led by CEO Sandy Weill, Citigroup in the past few years has created in its Corporate and Investment Banking Group (CIB) the leading contender for Goldman Sachs' leadership.

Citigroup's strength as an embedded player in key emerging markets like Poland, Mexico and Asia, along with the balance sheet of the world's largest financial institution, gives it a global reach unique in the

Figure 10.1   Citigroup's equity capital base dominates the sector (in $bn as of end 2001)

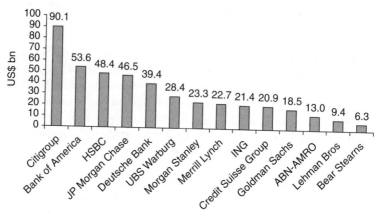

Source: Citigroup and company data (data as of 1Q02 except HSBC, UBS Warburg, Merrill Lynch, ING, Crédit Suisse Group which are as of 4Q01). Includes common and preferred equity, as well as parent and subsidiary trust and redeemable preferred securities.

commercial banking world. Figure 10.1 compares its capital strength with those of its peers.

By blending successfully Smith Barney's retail brokerage business, Salomon's debt and other capabilities, and Schroder's corporate finance skills, the merged group now has the product range which the commercial bank lacked. Figure 10.2 depicts the scope of the group's product capabilities and geographical coverage.

Thus in 2001 Citigroup could boast of having become the leading global underwriter in combined debt and equity with a 12 per cent market share, as well a leading global investment bank with its 7 per cent share of the global fee pool. In Japan, its alliance with Nikko Cordial was the leading equity bookrunner. In global equities and completed M & A, however, the group ranked third and fifth, respectively. Citi's CIB accounted for 53 per cent of the group's 2001 profits.

Citigroup has used its balance sheet to great effect in winning debt and other mandates by skilfully employing its lending power. While this implies some degree of margin subsidization, the group's risk control systems seem to have minimized the asset quality problems which have beset the JP Morgan merger.

The operational model underpinning this colossus is equally rare. Driven by a strong leader in the person of CEO Sandy Weill, Citigroup has a rigorous cost-management culture, is relatively risk-averse, and

Figure 10.2   Citigroup's product and geographical scope

Unique Platform	Smith Barney	Salomon Brothers	Citibank	Nikko	Schroders	Combined
Equity sales & trading	●	◐	○	◑	◐	●
Fixed income sales & trdg	○	●	○	◑	○	●
Investment banking	◐	◐	○	◐	◐	●
Municipals	●	○	○	○	○	●
Foreign exchange	○	○	●	○	○	●
Structured products	○	○	●	○	○	●
Lending	○	○	●	○	○	●
Cash & trade	○	○	◑	○	○	●
Securities services	○	○	◑	○	○	◑
Retail distribution	●	○	○	●	○	●
U.S.	◐	◐	◐	○	○	●
Europe	○	◑	◐	○	◐	◑
Emerging markets	○	◑	◑	○	○	●
Japan	○	◑	○	●	○	●

● Leading   ◑ Strong   ◐ Moderate   ○ Weak

has shown a rare ability to blend different banking cultures with minimal loss of key professionals. As discussed above in Chapter 5, the model incorporates a client coverage approach which diverges from the Goldman ideal but seems to be making progress.

Some of the comments from our interview sample reflect this success:

"They are winning mandates with their combined CIB model" – Nordea

"Sandy Weill is obsessed with cost control" – Boston Consulting Group

"They're continually questioning what they do; they're the most driven people I've ever seen" – Greenwich Associates

"Citi has both the balance sheet and the bull terrier mentality" – Lehman Brothers

"Sandy Weill is the real winner (in the acquisition game)" – JP Morgan

"Sandy Weill seems to walk on water." – NM Rothschild

"Citi is on the way to becoming the truly global investment bank; and Sandy has an incredible eye on the dollar." – First Consulting

"They have the products, but not yet the client model" – Morgan Stanley

"Another success story for multiple acquirers." – Lehman Brothers

The CIB function's challenges are twofold. First, can the world's largest financial institution actually execute its strategy of intense client coverage across multiple products, geographies and client segments? Will their framework of dual coverage, with its inevitable overlaps and ambiguities, compete successfully with more focused rivals?

Managing Director David Bowerin, who has played a major role in developing the new framework, is confident:

> *"Our clients like it and because of this it produces good results. We also have a code of conduct and rules of the road which provide guidelines on appropriate behaviour. For us, the concept has legs!"*

A related issue is whether the group can convince its target clients to desert traditional investment bankers like Goldman Sachs and Morgan Stanley for the prized M & A and equities mandates. Sir Win Bischoff describes the challenge:

> *"The great advantage of the group will be when the various mergers are bedded down and you can develop a service-oriented culture with extremely competent people. We're not there yet, but when we are you won't be able to tell the Citigroup man in the room from the guy from Goldman or JP Morgan."*

Once again, we shall address these issues in the final two chapters.

Morgan Stanley Dean Witter: blending strong corporate discipline with a diversified product array

While a close number two to Goldman Sachs in the strategically important M & A and equities businesses, Morgan Stanley has also successfully diversified into retail brokerage, fund management and the credit card business to offset its reliance on investment banking products. The result is what Brad Hintz of Sanford Bernstein, and a former Morgan Stanley Treasurer, terms

> *"a champion in the decathlon ... the best all-around athlete on the field today."*

Thus in Europe the firm in 2001 ranked in the top two in equities, M & A and international bonds, and over a five-year period figured among the top three in four key businesses.

The merger with Dean Witter provided the group with the retail distribution strength of about 14,000 retail brokers, while the firm's asset management business runs about $600 million in client assets and accounts for about 10 per cent of the firm's revenues. Its Discover credit card accounts for roughly 17 per cent of its global revenues. Abroad, overseas earnings represent about 26 per cent of total revenue, with strong brokerage and fund management businesses in the UK, Spain, Italy and other European markets.

In 2001, the firm earned an impressive 19 per cent ROE, down from a remarkable 31 per cent in the banner year 2000, and well above the average of the US bulge group. Its equity base of $23 billion situates Morgan Stanley between Citigroup and Goldman Sachs, with a corresponding ability to lend money to support its investment banking mandates.

Another defining characteristic of the firm is its disciplined management focus, which is reflected in relatively high margins, good expense control, low risk preference and strong management controls. Fitch notes that its pre-tax net income has had the lowest volatility in its peer group for the decade to 2001.

The firm's compensation/revenue ratio of 47.3 per cent in 2001 was the lowest of its US peers. Its IT investment has produced results: Figure 10.3 shows how the firm has been able to drive down unit costs by over 50 per cent in recent years.

Figure 10.3   Morgan Stanley institutional securities trading volume and cost per trade

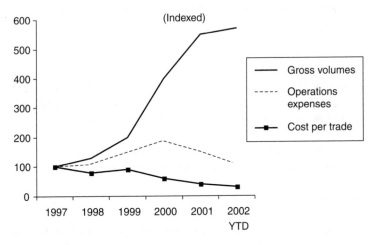

Source: Morgan Stanley.

Amelia Fawcett explains how the firm in Europe has disaggregated some of its back-office functions to reduce costs:

"All of us have legacy problems in IT and clearance and settlement. We set up a task force to look at the issues and possible solutions. We found that for some businesses and processes we could break down what seemed to be a monolithic back-office structure into discrete parts."

Morgan Stanley's operational model has many of the same features as that of Goldman but is generally seen as less intense – 'a more comfortable place to work' – and arguably more oriented to serve its clients' needs than some of its competitors. It also has two cultures which, as indicated in Chapter 4, generate a certain amount of conflict to offset the obvious synergies between wholesale and retail investment banking.

The comments from our survey reflect these operational features:

"Everywhere I go in Europe it's Morgan Stanley" – Dresdner Kleinwort Wasserstein

"Morgan Stanley is best at structuring risk management with strong senior management support" – Fitch

"I was wrong when I said that Morgan Stanley couldn't manage size" – Harvard Business School

"They do what's good for the client" – JP Morgan

"They're more genteel than Goldman Sachs" – Lehman Brothers

"top of the list in strategic thinking" – JP Morgan

"the most attractive culture" – UBS

For the two Morgan Stanley executives interviewed, the challenges for the future are generic: keep executing the medium-term strategy, cut costs and build people strength. In Amelia Fawcett's words:

"It's a question of not losing our vision of the medium term outlook. We need to keep the ship stable, focus on clients and build our people strength."

Donald Moore adds one more point:

"We need to reinforce our culture – to keep people focused on the value of working in an investment bank. With all the focus on compensation, one

tends to lose sight of the very substantial psychic income, meeting and working with great people, working on challenging assignments, and assisting clients in achieving their objectives."

If there is another issue, it is that posed by rivalry between the group's retail and wholesale functions. The political struggle highlighted by John Mack's departure may reflect an understandable cultural divide between the retail and wholesale businesses. And in the context of heightened competition from balance sheet-rich banks like Citigroup, the capital committed to the Discover card franchise might be better applied to other purposes.

The divide is noted by Moore:

"While there's some overlap between retail and investment banking, they are really quite separate businesses, which overlap like olympic circles. Each can benefit from the strengths of the others but you need to manage the interface to realise the benefits."

Other case studies of success

Successful business models in investment banking are not exclusive to the three firms discussed above and their global peers. Having absorbed the barrage of statistics and strategic ambitions validating the presumably superior models of the global bulge group, we asked our friends whether the middle ground of investment banking – firms somewhere between the globals and the advisory boutiques – could constitute a viable business model.

The following four case studies seem to indicate that such models can not only exist but also thrive. In the final two chapters we explore the possible extent of this prosperity in the future. At this point, however, we invite the reader to examine these case studies with a view to the future of the shape of the industry and the critical success factors which will drive it.

Lehman Brothers: a return from the grave driven by disciplined diversification

In 1994, following a near-collapse of its partnership in the mid-1980s and a turbulent period under the ownership of American Express, Lehman Brothers was floated on the New York Stock Exchange just in time to be buffeted by the worst collapse in years of its core product, fixed-income origination and trading. Pundits once again pronounced its certain death – or at least acquisition by a larger competitor.

Instead the firm has become a role model for disciplined diversification in terms of cost control, internationalization, penetration of more profitable product segments and risk management. Under the leadership of Dick Fuld, its CEO who was a fixed-income executive during the firm's problem years in the mid-1980s, Lehman has achieved a level of ROE fully competitive with its peers, a cost-income ratio which is the envy of the business and the almost universal admiration from competitors. Lehman boasts the highest – 23 per cent per annum – growth in revenues and level of pre-tax margins – 28 per cent – of its US peers over the five-year period ended in 2001.

While Lehman did not figure in our straw poll rankings, the firm received many unsolicited compliments from our interview sample. For example:

> *"Lehman eats structured deals"* – JP Morgan Chase

> *"Lehman shows how difficult it is to destroy a good franchise!"* – Citigroup

> *"Lehman won't go away"* – Nomura

Fixed income remains one of the firm's core businesses, but Lehman has moved from traditional proprietary trading to the higher margin structured or leveraged deals in which, according to one observer, it *'slices, dices and repackages products'*.

But the strategic goal is to build a diversified quintet of products and markets, termed 'crop rotation' at the firm: investment banking, equities, private clients, private equity and Europe. Lehman has built its equities trading business successfully in both Europe and the US to move well into the top ten league. Overseas earnings – primarily Europe – account for over 40 per cent of total revenues, with Lehman having hired teams in markets like Italy to drive its investment banking business.

Investment banking – in particular M & A – remains the major challenge, with the firm still outside the top ten globals and probably earning a sub-par single-digit ROE on the business. The number of investment banking professionals has more than doubled since 1998 to an estimated 2200 today, supported by over 600 analysts. The fragmented European market is a key strategic priority.

What captures the attention of most competitors, however, is Lehman's success in cost management, which we described earlier in

Chapter 8. Lehman has the lowest ratio of non-personnel expenses to net revenues – 21 per cent in 2001 – as well as a compensation/net revenues ratio which has remained steady at 51 per cent in recent years. Its former CFO, Brad Hintz of Sanford Bernstein, terms this *'the strongest record of expense control in the history of the securities industry'*.

The firm's future, as it has been for years, is a constant topic of conversation. Will Lehman be able to break into the sun-lit uplands of the M & A world? Can it succeed in the fragmented and highly competitive European market? And will the management team decide to cash out, as the DLJ team did in 2000? Management ownership of the stock has soared from 4 per cent in 1994 to 33 per cent currently, and boosting this percentage is a key priority.

One can opine on these fascinating issues, but from our standpoint the case study of Lehman illustrates several key points.

First, the human dynamic of investment banking has demonstrated how a firm can come back from the grave to become a successful role model in a number of critical success factors. Whatever the future holds for Lehman, the story can be repeated by others with the requisite credentials: strong and determined leadership, the acquisition of skilled professionals, a sensible diversification strategy, and above all superb execution, both in terms of cost and risk management as well as client work.

The case study also reflects the dynamic which pushes a successful investment bank to extend its reach to new products and markets. As we discussed in the case of DLJ, committed and creative professionals do not stand still when they perceive growth opportunities. Lehman now finds itself, like so many larger firms, up against the formidable competition of the investment banking oligopoly in M & A. And it has to make some difficult choices in the European market against equally tough competition.

In sum, the ultimate fate of Lehman Brothers will be a most intriguing chapter in the evolution of investment banking in the years to come!

Carnegie Group: a classic geographic focus for an independent bank

Another independent investment bank spun out of a larger parent, Carnegie Group has succeeded in maintaining a leadership position in the Nordic investment banking sector with number one ranking in number of deals done for the all-important M & A and equities businesses in 2001.

Having been sold during the Swedish banking crisis by the troubled Nordbanken (now Nordea) and ultimately floated on the Stockholm stock exchange in 2001, Carnegie is one of the rare regional investment banking successes in a world dominated either by the globals or by much smaller local specialists. While Carnegie now focuses entirely on Nordic-related clients and transactions, it abandoned a pan-European strategy during the 1990s by divesting strong local businesses in the Iberian Peninsula and Italy. As CEO Lars Bertmar acknowledges:

"We're arrogant enough to say to our clients 'We'll give you our speciality but you'll have to go elsewhere for other products'."

Carnegie received in our interview series the ultimate accolade from its competitors – unreserved praise. As Handelsbanken's Göran Björling puts it:

"Carnegie has the 'magic!' It took them 12 years to do it: slowly and methodically."

Underpinning Carnegie's business model is the central role of market definition, or 'niche' in today's vocabulary. For Bertmar, everything depends on the size and share of the chosen market:

"What is 'mid-sized'? In a way, it's very easy. You have to strive to be the leader. If you're close – say number one, two or three – to lead in a niche, you're a large player in that niche. It all depends on the size of the niche. Goldman Sachs is 20 times our size but it's still in a niche – the large cap globals. It's the same story for them: Goldman strives to be the leader in its segment. There's lots of misunderstanding about being 'global' or 'pan-Euro'. You risk becoming a number 10 or 15 with a huge cost base and larger and larger losses. You have to define the niche in which you're a leader to make sense. It is risky! Maybe the Nordic niche will be risky, but the market is big enough. There's always a place for a leader, but none for a number seven!"

Apart from a profitable asset management and private banking business, Carnegie's product focus is exclusively M & A and equity capital markets. Its ROE of 38 per cent in the down year of 2001 compares with an even more remarkable 85 per cent in the peak year of 2000. Its share of trading on the Nordic exchanges was 8 per cent in 2001 – the same as its portion of the volume of Nordic M & A.

While the firm originally focused on medium-sized clients and trans-actions, it now can play a role as 'the best colleague to the globals' as a co-lead manager with strong local distribution and insights. Although Carnegie tops the league tables in terms of the number of deals, it is generally pushed down the volume rankings by global firms executing the larger mandates.

Sustaining this business model is a strong entrepreneurial culture as well as the unique 50/50 bonus formula described in Chapter 6. The result is a cost base which Bertmar believes compares favourably with that of its peers, and a compensation/revenue ratio of 50 per cent. He describes a Goldman Sachs-type culture that is

> *"Extremely business-oriented with an apolitical, unbureaucratic client focus. The ten themes of our culture are instilled in the heads of all new employees. We call it 'guerrilla warfare,' not an army! It's important that everyone is clear about the rules and values we share."*

Bertmar sees the challenge for the future as maintaining Carnegie's share of a growing Nordic market. The short-term outlook is gloomy and Carnegie's outsized ROE is under threat, but the business model in our view is sound.

The lesson of the Carnegie case study is to reaffirm the point made by CEO Bertmar: it is the size of the relevant market, rather than general-izations such as globality, and one's share of that market which determines the validity of an investment banking business model. Can Carnegie retain that share in the face of competition from both the globals as well as universal banks like SEB and SHB? The evidence to date is that it can – if it retains its entrepreneurial culture and continues to attract and retain superior professionals.

Macquarie Bank Limited: a domestic leader succeeds abroad in well-defined specialities

Macquarie Bank is one of the rare instances in which a domestic banking leader has been able to translate local skills into a global leadership position – specifically in the infrastructure finance and equity deriva-tives sectors.

Having emerged in the mid-1980s from the former Australian branch of the UK merchant bank Hill Samuel, Macquarie is now publicly held.

Figure 10.4   Future direction of Macquarie's international expansion

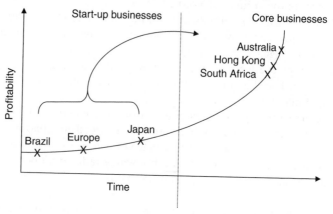

Source: Macquarie Bank.

Its ROE in 2001 was an impressive 27 per cent, which continues a string of annual earnings increases with ROEs well above 20 per cent.

It ranks among the leaders in the Australian M & A and equities sectors, with a top five position in each of the past five years and a number two ranking in equities issuance in 2000. Outside the investment banking realm the firm is active in asset management and retail financial services. A unique dimension of the model is the 32 per cent of revenues constituted by contractual or annuity income from funds managed.

Macquarie's unique achievement, however, is to build on its expertise as a leader in Australian asset-based finance (essentially for infrastructure and other projects) and equity derivatives to expand abroad. Figure 10.4 describes the evolution of its international expansion, which now accounts for 38 per cent of group profits. Thus in Hong Kong as well as South Africa, Macquarie is the leader in warrant issuance as well as other derivative-based equity products.

Another dimension of its international expansion is the successful use of the joint venture structure in which Macquarie provides expertise and the domestic partner its client base and local insight. In South Africa the firm has two such ventures: one with the Sanlam insurance group for innovative retail investment products and the other with Standard Bank for commodity finance and structured finance. A Japanese joint venture has also been established with the Mizuho banking group. In markets like the UK, Macquarie has used its infrastructure expertise to take equity positions in major projects such as Bristol Airport.

The 'loose/tight' culture which supports this strategy was discussed in Chapter 4. A bonus plan driven by returns above the cost of capital is an integral part of the performance-oriented Macquarie operating model.

What are the challenges faced by Macquarie, in particular in its international expansion? Investment banking head Nicholas Moore gives his forecast:

> *"We're under no illusion that people will deal with us because we're Macquarie; we have to demonstrate value added. But we're pretty relaxed about the future. It comes back to the individual. Each professional realizes he has to do better or he won't get paid. If we offer the same product as Deutsche Bank, Deutsche Bank will get the business. We have to be more adventurous, more open-minded. We deal with people where we can make a difference – where capital is the most important variable. We keep asking: how can we maximize the value for our clients, investors and the Bank? The goal is to make money – not doing the same thing you did last year."*

Will the model stand up? The answer is very similar to our reflections on Carnegie: if the entrepreneurial culture can be maintained and Macquarie continues to innovate in competition with formidable global competitors, the future is bright. At home, the firm is the only indigenous financial institution to compete successfully with these rivals. Abroad, the challenge is arguably greater, but the same critical success factors apply.

Cazenove: a survivor from 'Big Bang' retains not only its independence but also leadership in UK equities

Another mid-sized investment bank to have survived the onslaught of US competitors as well as the restructuring of the British financial sector is Cazenove, the dominant UK equity underwriter and a leader in M & A as well.

From its origins as a UK 'company broker' – essentially acting as an interface between issuers and the equity markets – Cazenove has successfully converted itself from an agency broker into an investment bank with a full advisory and equity markets capability. Over the five years to 2001, the firm has ranked first in UK equity bookrunning with strength in both the large as well as small and mid-cap sectors – defying the conventional wisdom that global players should dominate the major deals. In addition, Cazenove ranked seventh in UK M & A in 2001. While it has an overseas network and covers European as well as UK securities, the bank remains largely dependent on its unique

UK franchise. Its advisory group of about 65 professionals is supported by about 400 in the secondary equities sector, including about 140 analysts.

While its UK peers all disappeared as independent entities, Cazenove retained its partnership structure after Big Bang in 1986 as well as its market position. CEO Robert Pickering attributes its success to sustaining client relationships rather than any unique strategy or business model:

> *"I'm not persuaded by the simplistic notion of global killers and smaller specialists. What has kept us going? It's very simple: if you provide a valuable service to clients they'll pay for it. Many of the larger banks have found themselves in trouble through over-strategizing. Success for us is a very loyal client base which goes back 25–30 years – the continuity of relationship and trust as well as our ability to attract the right people to manage the relationship. Our cultural roots are primarily in stockbroking rather than merchant banking which means we are less hierarchical, not grand and have people who are nice to work with."*

By late 2000, with roughly 1100 employees and 80 partners, Cazenove decided to convert to limited company status and float before April, 2003. Being able to offer stock to a wide range of employees has been a key driver in this decision. Robert Pickering summarizes his thinking on the issue of compensation:

> *"Under the partnership there was a 'winner-take-all' situation with no ability to extend ownership to a larger number. People don't work just for money; if you rely on that alone, you can never win, since there's always someone who can offer more. So you rely on a compelling overall program: being part of a winning team, doing interesting work, and having a fair compensation package. We have a single firm-wide profit pool which pays out quarterly. Essentially everyone is a stockholder – a friendly, mutually supportive atmosphere, a nice place to work."*

Can this unique culture survive the public markets? Pickering was quoted in a *Financial Times* article as follows:

> *"If you get to the point where your structure defines you, your culture isn't very robust."*[42]

Apart from the challenges of dealing with the new structure, we would guess that cost management will be a major preoccupation for Cazenove's leadership. As Pickering points out:

> *"The partnership concept focused on providing income for the partners, not maximizing profits, and there was comparatively little in the way of cost control."*

Another issue may be Cazenove's international dimension. While the firm has 12 offices outside the UK, Pickering sets out his international objective as follows:

> *"While in no way diminishing the importance of our other international businesses, in five years we would like to be known as a 'strong European investment bank'. Our international model will be the same as in the UK: independent advice supported by strong distribution."*

These case studies across the investment banking landscape illustrate how business and operational models can succeed in a variety of markets ranging from the global to the regional and the local.

Others could have been selected as well. The former DLJ was cited by a number of our friends as having built a highly successful mid-sized business around a number of specialities in which the firm held a leadership position. Barclays Capital also gets high marks for having built a profitable debt-led business from a commercial banking base. Fox-Pitt Kelton, now owned by Swiss Re, is unique in having specialized profitably in a single sector – financial institutions – with its package of independent research, sales and trading, and M & A.

The list could go on. But the lessons learned from the three global and four regional/specialist competitors should be sufficient to enable us to evaluate the outlook in the final two chapters.

11
Views for the Future

"Everybody has got to change somewhat to make it to the promised land."

– Jim Freeman, Freeman & Co.

"It's a misconception that everyone wants to imitate Goldman Sachs."

– Lars Grönstedt, SHB

'What does your crystal ball show for the outlook of your business' was the final question to our interview sample. More specifically, our intent was to engage them in a discussion of the intermediate term: how might the investment banking business change over the next three to five years in terms of structure, profitability, strategies, management priorities, and other key issues.

The short term was not of interest to us, partly because it will be largely over by the time this book is published, but also because the business by nature is volatile, with cycles which are extraordinarily difficult to predict.

But it was clear to many of our friends that this short-term outlook would play a major role in driving the long-term profile. Several interviewees thus offered two medium-term forecasts: one based on a reasonably quick recovery in volumes and therefore profits, or an extended revenue drought which would be more likely to drive structural change. A typical response was that of Bob Yates of Fox-Pitt Kelton:

"The key to the future is the level of activity. The last 20 years have been exceptional ones for investors. If market activity and returns diminish, the number of salesmen and analysts which you need to support this will decline. In that scenario, there will be more consolidation with fewer

people and firms. Both primary and secondary market activity could be affected. The number of mega deals could fall, and you'd have a greater proportion of smaller deals – essentially tidying up – and more deals done in-house. Lower margins would be part of the picture as there would be even more excess capacity."

Nicholas Coulson agrees:

"If we have a serious deflation as a result of the stock market bubble, etc. we could be looking into the abyss: we will have seen nothing yet in terms of cost cuts! But if you believe in a normal recovery, with gradual change, there's going to be some more consolidation in Europe along the lines of what happened in the US."

Maureen Erasmus, head of European strategy at Lehman Brothers, cautions against an over-sanguine view of the nature of the business:

"You can't assume that market corrections are infrequent; they're here to stay, say every two to three years. The highs and lows are longer, with more volatility. Capital, not trade flows, will drive the economics. Market change won't happen as fast as we'd like in areas such as cross-border settlements because of vested interests."

Putting aside for the moment this key driver of cyclical timing, let's first address the issues on which there is general agreement.

Most interviewees acknowledge that significant overcapacity was built up over the late 1990s and would have a significant impact on the business' future. They differ, however, in how impact would be felt.

Most believe that margins are likely on balance to continue to decline. Figure 11.1 summarizes our interpretation of the drivers cited for such a decline.

Certainly a straightforward projection of recent trends would justify such a view. Figure 3.9 in Chapter 3 tracked margins in four key products in the US market, and we understand that the same pattern exists in Europe and other markets, albeit starting from a lower base.

For example, Huw van Steenis of JP Morgan Chase, citing his survey on European equity trading conducted with McKinsey & Co., forecasts:

"The economics of the equities business will approach that of the debt markets with thinner margins. In particular, the economics of the mid-sized players will be hit."

Figure 11.1 Most trends point to further margin pressure

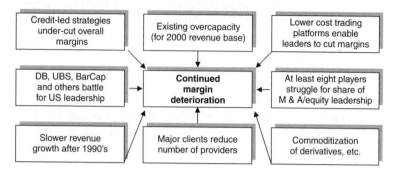

Several observers note a likely convergence of returns from commercial and investment banking as a result of the fierce competition for investment banking market share. Thus a senior London-based executive points out:

> *"Investment banking is overbanked like commercial banking; it has to change."*

A recent McKinsey study notes that ROEs in investment banking could fall by 30 per cent driven in large part by the credit-led strategies of the large universal banks.[38] Mark Williams of McKinsey comments:

> *"A 15% post-tax ROE may not be bad in a low interest environment for large universal banks."*

Per-Anders Ovin of Enskilda Securities, which has been hard hit by the decline in the Nordic equities markets, opines that

> *"It's going to be very rough. The problem is that investment banking as a business is like a derivative on the underlying market. There's a recovery now, but the upside periods will be shorter. Over everything there is the layer of overcapacity, which will lead to lower fees. The same critical success factor is still there – the exponential relationship between market share and profitability. A lower level of profits will reduce the number of players. At the same time those of us who are left will have to cut capacity, but it won't be enough. ROEs will be hurt."*

There is also a consensus that revenue growth will slow after the heady days of the TMT boom in the late 1990s. From compound annual rates during the 1990s of 10–20 per cent depending on the sector, a world of single-digit volume increases is forecast, with pessimists closer to 5–6 per cent per annum growth.

In Europe, for example, many believe that the major movement in equitization – the shift to greater equity ownership – is now past, along with the surge in retail demand triggered by the technology bubble. On the other hand, the official stance of all the global banks is that revenue-generating prospects in Europe are the most attractive of any major market.

While the pace may slow, there is little doubt in the minds of our interview sample that investment banking remains a growth business. Peter Weinberg of Goldman Sachs is optimistic but has a few caveats:

> *"Investment banking has good growth prospects. The risk of being wrong in the capital markets is so high that there will always be a role for good advice and for a broad range of products. You can still have 8–10 players at the top. But no one in the business can rest on his laurels; we get challenged every day. The question is whether one or two will pull away and distance themselves from the pack. But if times remain tough, some will panic."*

Lars Bertmar of Carnegie is another who remains resolutely optimistic about the business, but repeats the caveat of Per-Anders Ovin about the issue of market share:

> *"Carnegie is built on the assumption that in the long run the industry will grow and provide a growing revenue stream. Given that, there will be winners and losers like any other industry. The winners will develop a franchise among the top three."*

Optimism for the long term is particularly prevalent among German bankers who have been awaiting the promised explosion in corporate restructuring, pension savings and conversion from bank to capital market finance. One such executive maintains that a higher stock price level will trigger the release of a major backlog of deals:

> *"We're at the low point of the business cycle, but there's great potential in all sectors. There's a big backlog of business; spin-offs will occur when [market] prices are higher."*

The great majority of those who opined on the future structure of the industry are convinced that consolidation will continue. Marcel Ospel, Walter Gubert, Don Moore, Huw van Steenis, Sir Win Bischoff, Ray Soifer, Robert Colthorpe, Svilen Ivanov, Nick Coulson, Mark Garvin, Nick O'Donohoe and Assaad Razzouk all see mergers involving the top global firms in the sector. If there is a consensus among them, it is that the present eight global bulge group players will be reduced to perhaps five or six in the intermediate term.

More specifically, they cite the following forces driving consolidation:

"The revenue pool from large corporates is not big enough to support profitable growth of the eight global players" – Svilen Ivanov

"There's excess capacity everywhere – too much capital, too many people" – Donald Moore

"Four–five truly global, fully-integrated firms" – Mark Garvin

"Consolidation isn't finished; Goldman Sachs and Morgan Stanley must do deals" – Nick O'Donohoe

And perhaps most poignant of all is the frank comment of one senior European investment banker with a mid-sized firm:

"There will be more consolidation, and we'll be part of it [as a seller!]"

The consensus starts to fray when the focus turns to the mass of competitors below the global bulge group.

In practice, this means the European universal banks outside the bulge group who are committed to some form of investment banking activity for their core clients. A host of labels have been pinned on them: national champions, 'deep country specialists', mid-sized banks, 'glocals', 'multi-specialists', mini-wholesale banks and pan-Euro institutions. But their common challenge is to survive in the middle ground between the globals and smaller specialists.

Few of our sources offered much in the way of positive encouragement over the long term for this segment. Figure 2.2 in Chapter 2 buttresses their argument: the share of the global investment banking fee pool taken by the US and the three European globals (Deutsche Bank, UBS Warburg and CSFB) has steadily eroded the share of all other players – largely the mid-sized banks – from 76 per cent to 54 per cent over the period 1993–2001.

Most of our interviewees thus subscribe to the 'dumb-bell' concept: one either benefits from size and scale as a large firm or from flexibility and entrepreneurship as a very small one. And in the more difficult operating environment described above, there will be losers, and the mid-sized competitors are almost unanimously assigned this unfortunate role.

A number of our interviewees, however, were more optimistic, pointing to the natural strengths of many of these banks and the progress they are making to revamp their business and operational models. Martin Smith, who has observed the evolution of the business over several decades, offers his advice:

> "*Don't give up hope; you don't need to be Godzilla! What's happened is that to get bigger, people created an enormous overhead, which forced them to concentrate on elephant hunting. When business was weak, they fell back on the middle market because they needed the business. The minimum fee size was $1 to 1.5 million, which left lots of deals of less than $1 million for others. The rhetoric got overheated. But boutiques will push into capital markets as well as the advisory business. There are lots of potential partners to help with the capital markets side; one just needs to build relationships with these partners.*"

Our Scandinavian friends in particular resent being forced into arbitrary boxes. Lars Grönstedt, CEO of SHB, objects:

> "*It's a misconception that everyone wants to imitate Goldman Sachs and that, if they can't or won't, that they've failed from the outset. In our experience, we have a very profitable investment bank without these ambitions!*"

Per-Anders Ovin of Enskilda Securities agrees:

> "*I've never believed that there's only one investment model – it's all about implementation. Lots of bulge group banks don't get it together. Scale is not an end in itself. The service level is defined by the client.*"

Assaad Razzouk expresses a common view that talent, not size, will be the differentiating factor:

> "*There's room for more than just four to five universal banks. It's a people business. If you have good people who are bright and can build good relationships, how can you lose?*"

Mark Williams of McKinsey is more specific:

> *"In M & A and equities, you can make a case for the survival of large national players. Here the proposition will be different from the large bulge group. The top 1000 stocks, for example, are well covered by the bulge group. This leaves a lot of room for small and mid-caps – a business which can be profitable. When you include the servicing of domestic institutions and the banks' own retail business, the numbers can add up.*
>
> *You'll be under threat for the largest clients, and it will be a small business compared to the revenues made by the bulge group, and you need to manage it with a clear focus on costs."*

Another beacon of hope comes from Richard Ramsden of Goldman Sachs for what he terms 'best of breed locals':

> *"The 'glocals' [global and local at the same time] are having a tough time. What is their competitive advantage? Perhaps the most successful are being local in their domestic market and perhaps global in a few niches – like Société Générale in derivatives. But the model has to be clearly defined, more clear-cut than most banks realize. And the market needs to move in your favour, since the globals can increasingly offer a better portfolio effect. Products follow a natural product cycle, and you can't be a single product firm. Local banks which are truly local can survive – being close to the market and offering a bespoke service, such as research on small companies."*

Roy Smith, a professor of finance at the Stern School of Business, speaks from his experience as a former Goldman Sachs partner in London:

> *"For the European so-called 'national champions', the wholesale business has gone multi-national where their championships don't mean anything. Most of these banks dominate the retail business in their countries, but lose their hold on corporate clients when they cross over into capital markets where the banks lack the ability to keep up with the global investment banks. Large US regional banks have this problem too. They focus on middle market companies, selling traditional banking products. But as the client becomes big enough to access capital markets (something that is easier to do all the time), the bank loses them to the investment banks. Or, to hang on to the clients they make expensive acquisitions of boutique investment banks (like Alex Brown, Robertson Stephens, Montgomery Securities, and Donaldson Lufkin) in order to be able to take them public or offer them*

junk bond financing. But the difficulties of managing the acquisitions have been so great, the strategies have rarely worked."

Will there be a return to the dominance of the geography function which would play to the strength of the nationally-based banks? Robert Statius-Muller thinks there might:

> *"There's a pendulum effect in investment banking. Today the global industry sectoral model is dominant. But I have to wonder: won't we go back in the direction of country knowledge, a more balanced view of industry and geography? If the global players continue to focus on the top firms in global sectors, might they lack critical mass in some of these segments? Take autos, for example. If you target only eight of the 200 firms globally in the business, can you afford a guy in every auto market? Maybe someone else in Germany can do a better job of servicing BMW."*

Another issue on which some consensus exists is that of aligning stockholder objectives and compensation levels. For academics as well as management, the issue posed by multi-million dollar packages for a wide range of talent is the most crucial one posed by the 1990s market effervescence.

Professor Sam Hayes of the Harvard Business School gives top priority to the resolution of this conflict:

> *"Is public ownership of investment banks appropriate? The culture of the public company is different from a partnership. Warren Buffett was thinking like a stockholder and tried (unsuccessfully) to address the problem of return to Salomon Brothers stockholders vs. compensation to the current management generation. There'll be a point at which the investment community says 'the emperor has no clothes: the firm is unprofitable, why do you pay bonuses?'"*

His concern is echoed by chief executives who have to manage the business. Adrian Evans of Lazard expressed a common view:

> *"How long can a cadre of people earn great multiples of the compensation of other professionals?"*

But the combined efforts of top management, the use of standard bonus formulae, and the action of the market itself seem to be reducing the problem to manageable proportions. The continued revenue drought, particularly in the high-profile M & A and primary equity sectors, has both reduced the available bonus pool as well as the rationale for the professionals' demands.

More important, however, have been the efforts of management teams to redress the balance. CSFB is addressing its problem of inflated compensation costs, as CFO Dick Thornburgh explains:

> *"We create [phantom] stock within the investment banking business. We say 'The seat here is very valuable. You want to be here because of that seat – it's worth more than you are.' In 2000 anyone could make money. We need a good old-fashioned correction which breaks down the cost of goods sold [people!]. The environment is weak, and pricing power is shifting to the employer, not the employee."*

While there is no guarantee that the effervescence of the late 1990s will not return, the disciplines of established bonus formulae are in place in many banks. Mid-sized quoted firms like Macquarie and Carnegie have long-established formulae which ensure a minimum return to stock-holders.

Even more important, however, is the almost universal objective of maximizing share ownership by current and past professionals. This essentially addresses the alignment problem by largely eliminating it. Thus Lehman's efforts to increase its internal ownership above the present level of 33 per cent (up from only 4 per cent at the time of the public offering in 1994) and Deutsche Bank's well-publicized strategy of issuing options to achieve the same purpose should go a long way to resolve the problem.

Does it work? Will current and former professionals wearing their stockholder hats act any differently from that of an employee interested only in short-term payout? We don't know, but there is every chance that a former partner or retired professional in an investment bank might take a longer-term view of his holding than an individual looking to maximize his annual bonus.

The outlook for growth in the European market unites most of our sources. Seen particularly from the US investment banker's point of view, Europe is an emerging market waiting to be exploited further by their business and operating models. Figure 11.2 summarizes the argument as seen from the standpoint of Morgan Stanley.

Most of the investor presentations and research by the US banks, for example, compare the two markets on the basis of such benchmarks as

Figure 11.2 Morgan Stanley's view of Europe

- 'Equification'
- 'Debtification'
- Restructuring
- Pension reform
- Fiscal reform

Europe is one of our great global opportunities

Source: Morgan Stanley.

market capitalization/GDP, trading volumes as a percentage of market cap, and corporate debt as a percentage of the total. They conclude, almost invariably, that convergence will take place over a period of time to the benefit, not surprisingly, of intermediaries in the debt and equity markets. Adding to this the long-awaited creation of a single European capital market rather than the existing 15 or so national markets, plus the stimulus to equity ownership from pension reform, has propelled Europe to the top of many US firms' agendas.

JP Morgan's Walter Gubert summarizes the argument based on his long career experience in Europe:

"In Europe, the good news is that a fragmented market will become less so. For example, fixed income is different in each market, but with a more standard platform, costs will come down. We believe in one trading centre and lots of distribution centres. Over time, something will change in Europe. The US already has a more unified market with less fragmentation in each business line. It will take years, but Europe will increasingly resemble the US concentration model."

Within Europe, the German market appears particularly appetizing: Europe's largest economy, pension reform taking hold, a financial system to be rationalized, and, above all, the market potential represented by the potential restructuring and shift to capital market from bank finance of the massive *Mittelstand* industrial sector. Karl Dannenbaum of Lehman Brothers is particularly articulate about the potential:

"During the 1990s, Germany represented about 10% of European M & A fees despite having a third of its GDP; now it's 20–25%. So Germany has moved, and it will move further. Everybody is fighting for a piece of the

market – a must for any global investment bank. But that also makes the market extremely competitive, and not everybody here is profitable."

One of his German competiters expresses both hope and frustration:

"Our challenge is that we have too many good people who don't get a good flow of business. The machine is in place, and people who want to perform."

At Morgan Stanley, Amelia Fawcett summarizes a widespread view:

"Over the next three to five years, Europe will go through a period of extraordinary change. There'll be a bigger pie, although lower margins."

This is echoed by Merrill Lynch's senior planner Ron Carlson:

"The securities business globally has the best growth potential – say one and a half or twice the rate of GDP growth – and the potential for Europe is still attractive. Its realization has been held back by the market situation, but the fundamental drivers of growth are still very much intact, and there is still a huge amount of business to be done."

The consensus breaks apart completely in discussing the appropriate business model for the future: the advisory-led one against the debt-led strategy. The battle is thus joined between the two former US commercial banks (JP Morgan Chase and Citigroup) in one corner and the traditional US investment banks (in particular, Goldman Sachs and Morgan Stanley) in the other, with the other globals somewhere in between.

As indicated above, each side vigorously defends its model, with few concessions to the opposition. There is little point here in repeating the arguments made in the earlier chapter. What is interesting, however, is the debate this has provoked among independent outside observers such as rating agencies, bank analysts and management consultants.

One school of thought sees convergence of the two extremes – either through mergers or a common movement to the centre. Jim Freeman of consultants Freeman & Co. focuses on the issue of credit risk:

"Everybody has got to change somewhat to make it to the promised land. All of them have weaknesses. Goldman Sachs makes loans but not enough of them to have a diversified risk portfolio, while some universal banks

have too much crap on their books. The issue is how to cover the weaknesses they all have."

A common theme of much of this comment is that of relative differentiation and specialization – essentially a middle ground between the protagonists. Simon Harris of Oliver, Wyman & Co. is an author of a thoughtful report prepared with Morgan Stanley:[39]

> *"There's been a lot of talk about convergence of investment and commercial banking; we see divergence instead. If you look at the top eight players, you'll see a broad alignment along separate 'debt-led' and 'equity-led' models. They overlap vis-à-vis clients, but do not always compete head-to-head in all product areas!"*

Eileen Fahey of Fitch also sees the value of specialization:

> *"There really is a role for the independent firm. Who wants to buy a balance sheet with its high risk! Goldman and Morgan Stanley have lots of competition but will survive."*

Moving away from the debate on industry structure, we found widespread agreement on several management issues. One is the need for perfecting the client coverage model. When asked about their own management challenges for the future, this topic came top of the list for a wide range of banks, including both the globals like JP Morgan Chase and Citigroup and also the European universal banks.

Patrick Soulard of Société Générale cites this as one of his major challenges:

> *"We must develop an in-depth approach to client relationships to meet the competition. The relationship with clients is becoming more important, with the provider's need to sell more and the client's desire to narrow the number of suppliers."*

Breaking down product silos is a particular challenge for the European banks. One senior European bank executive expresses his deep concern:

> *"Now we're down in the last saloon: how to work across the product range."*

One of the most contentious issues is the related one of whether the global bulge group has indeed become too large and complex to manage effectively in the fast-moving investment banking world. Once again the battlelines are drawn up by the respective protagonists, and repeating their arguments here would add little value.

Perhaps independent academics, consultants and analysts can provide an objective view. Dwight Crane of the Harvard Business School offers his own thoughts:

> *"The pendulum will swing toward specialist firms – such as advisory and trading specialist products. 'Human-sized' firms will come back. You will be able to link activities without being part of the same firm. Look at Wasserstein Perella; they started as a boutique, but then began to add related businesses and grow."*

His colleague Sam Hayes puts the same argument against size in more colourful terms:

> *"It's like lemmings running over the cliff. You can't afford to be left behind. Everybody has bulked up. How big is big enough? When does it become a liability rather than a virtue? Size creates dead weight – like a 500 pound gorilla. He can swat a target in front of him, but if it flies around his head he can't reach it. We'll see the persistence of investment banks that are not huge but slough off bits around the edges and reconfigure themselves in a boutique form. Boutiques have done very well and will continue to do so, but some products obviously require deep pockets and the ability to absorb risk."*

For Guy Moszkowski, Salomon Smith Barney's investment banking analyst, the question is a very simple one: can they execute?

> *"We think success for both the 'interlopers' and the traditional investment banks will depend on their ability to execute, combining benefits of capital and skill sets without taking undue credit risk. Chances are, a couple of bank-affiliated firms will succeed; most others will not."*[40]

Richard Ramsden puts it a bit differently:

> *"Investment banking in five years will look a lot different from what it does today. In recent years everyone who had a pulse made money. In the future, the focus will be on thinking creatively about the business: different businesses working more closely together, developing new product ideas, and redeploying people from one business to another, getting more flexibility*

from the talent pool when one sector or business is down and others are booming. Each wave is different; you need to be flexible and nimble."

For Robert Colthorpe, it is time for the sector in Europe to rethink its strategies and processes after an unprecedented growth period:

"Investment banking is a growing business with more deals to be done and more markets to penetrate – becoming a feature of life as it has in the US. But it's been through a huge growth phase and sucked in people who have grown beyond their competence and organizations which have grown without thinking. The next two to three years will make people think harder about the business. A small number of bulge bracket firms will emerge but won't dominate; there will be lots of room for focused, geography-based players. The European banks like Société Générake and BNP Paribas will continue to operate and become large investment banking units. They should be better managed but less individualistic – fewer stars and more teams and processes."

In the next chapter, we opine ourselves on how flexible some of today's leaders might be, as well as some of the other issues touched on in this and previous chapters.

12
Our Own Views

Bitter experience, natural shyness and concern for professional reputation lead us away from hard predictions and toward the analysis of trends and issues. And we have already noted earlier the manifest inability of outsiders to fathom the workings of the investment banking world!

Yet the effort must be made. Having faithfully recorded the forecasts of some 50 practitioners and outside analysts over some six months of research, we must opine in particular on the views expressed in the previous chapter to preserve our sense of professional pride as bank analysts.

That said, we quickly posit our caveats. This volume will not see the light of day until early 2003, almost a year from the date of the earliest interviews. On the investment bankers' calendar, this constitutes a few aeons of time. Deals in all likelihood will be done, stars may become dogs, and new issues will surge to the fore. More specifically, when it comes to naming names and dates, we retreat into our cocoon, preferring to talk about trends and generic behaviours!

In sum, our philosophy is that one can add more predictive value in carefully analysing the present and past rather than making hard forecasts about the future. But here are some thoughts!

First, let's look at some independent projections to address the issue of market environment raised by some of the interviewees in Chapter 11. Figure 12.1 provides projections for the investment banking fee pool for the years 2002–03 made by Freeman & Co. on the basis of the firm's deep understanding of the business.

This data confirms the sustained nature of the retreat since the banner year of 2000 – clearly the high-water mark for investment banking for some time to come. The year 2003 is likely to show little growth over the two previous ones, with a projected fee pool of $36.6 billion, some

Figure 12.1   Projections for global fee pool to 2003 by geography (amounts in $ billions)

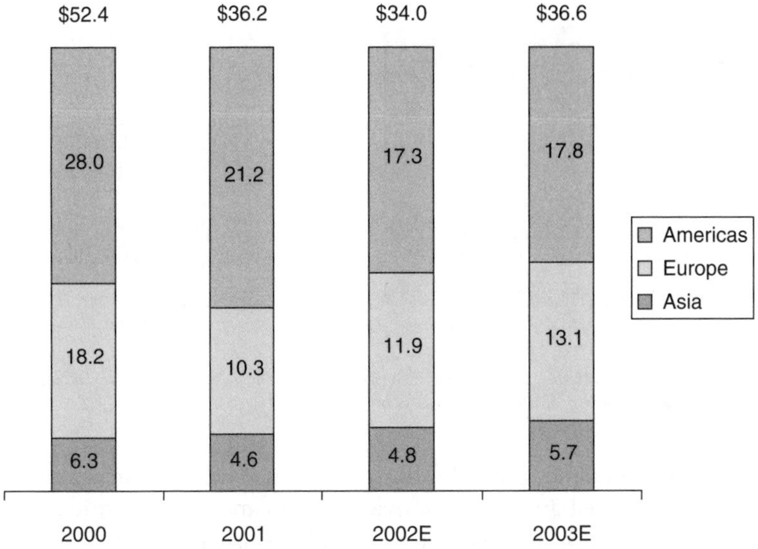

Source: Freeman & Co. projections as of 4/2002.

30 per cent below the 2000 record. Several longer-term industry projections depict a 'hockey stick' surge in 2004–05 to bring volumes back above the 2000 peak, but readers of investment banking research are painfully familiar with the sector's proclivity for such future acceleration!

When one combines this revenue forecast with the consensus of continued margin attrition indicated in the previous chapter, the outlook becomes bleaker for the business as a whole. Per the McKinsey/JP Morgan study cited above, margins in the secondary equity markets, one of the major profit contributors in both Europe and the US, will continue to slide as concentration continues apace and new, lower-cost trading platforms are installed.

In this context one of the major question marks is the profit outlook for derivatives, in particular equity derivatives. Accounting (as indicated in Figure 3.5) for perhaps a quarter of total sector profits, the higher margin segment of this rapidly evolving business has sustained the profitability of many banks in recent years. Figure 12.2, taken from the McKinsey & Co./JP Morgan study, would appear to indicate that derivatives account for roughly half of total equity and equity-related profits.

Figure 12.2   Equity-related revenue and profit by product for global players, 1999–2000 (indexed)[1]

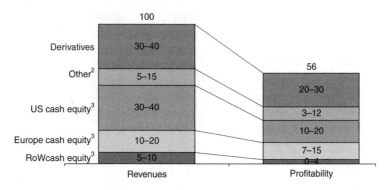

Sources: McKinsey estimates. 1. Selected global player sample. 2. Clearing and prime brokerage. 3. Includes a proportion of IPO sales concessions.

The business defies generalization, although clearly products such as capital-guaranteed funds, derivatives used to manage volatility, and credit derivatives have played a major role in driving its profitability. Can the profit record be maintained? The answer to this question will certainly be a major factor in the investment banking outlook.

In the absence of other factors (of which more below), the combination of sustained excess capacity, high fixed costs and margin pressure could do some damage to the industry's reputation for premium ROEs. This could lead to the consolidation of the business, as management teams cash out, or the withdrawal of capital in favour of alternatives such as asset management or retail banking.

In this context, it does not require a degree from a leading business school to predict that the trickle of layoffs of client-facing bankers as well as back office staff as of mid-2002 could become a flood. Assuming the pain of excess capacity does indeed stretch through the year 2003, one of our friends at JP Morgan Chase notes that '*in our bulimic industry, when the anchovies aren't flowing, you put people back on the street*'.

As for other costs, in particular technology and infrastructure, it is hard to envisage a sea change in the attitude toward outsourcing, joint ventures in back office functions, and generally making a root and branch assault on the cost base. Three years of revenue drought may well change behaviour, but the pressures to add costs to generate precious revenues are deeply entrenched in the culture.

One expense item that is likely to be high on the cost-cutting agenda is equity research. In particular, for those firms without either (or both) substantial investment banking earnings or retail distribution, carrying a massive complement of researchers largely to support the investment banking effort is difficult to justify.

More specifically, when one combines this profit pressure with the clearly expressed preference by institutions for a change in both content and delivery of research – quite apart from the separate current debate over transparency and objectivity – the drivers for the 'paradigm shift' cited by Marcel Ospel are powerful. Bankers with long memories will recall the good old days when brokerage research was highly valued by sales/trading staff as well as clients for its independence. Some of the survivors of those pre-Big Bang days are still around in the form of brokerages like Sanford Bernstein and Fox-Pitt Kelton, and they and others will hopefully prosper.

What might alter this prognosis? Certainly a revenue boost above the levels foreseen in Figure 12.1 would erase these concerns, and unexpected surges – such as the fixed income boom of 2001–02 – have historically come to the banks' rescue. New leadership can also play a role for individual firms, as the arrival of John Mack at CSFB and Bruce Wasserstein at Lazard seem to confirm. In contrast, individual firms like Drexel Burnham, the old Lehman and Barings have suddenly imploded for a variety of reasons.

What does all this mean for consolidation, the topic which comes top of mind to most of our interview sample? To us the most important factor is what drives this consolidation. Unlike the case of commercial banking, where the economics of in-market consolidation can be compelling, we see no economic law or force of nature which dictates this in the investment banking world.

Instead, future investment banking mergers are likely to take place between consenting adults, each of which is taking a bet on the future. The extended internal debate in former partnerships like Goldman Sachs and the sale of quoted companies like DLJ in 2000 confirms that investment bankers have a finely tuned sense of present and likely future value, in particular when it comes to realizing their own net worth!

As for the buyers, market share in target segments is likely to be the main driver. There are no prizes for identifying what these segments might be: positioning generally in the US, and the M & A/equity sectors targeted by so many relative newcomers to the global market.

Much more challenging is guessing which combinations might work in practice. Industry pundits delight in pairing commercial banks, with a massive balance sheet but a modest role in high-value investment banking products, with an investment bank partner who complements them neatly on paper. Such marriages totally ignore the lessons of experience in attempting to blend two totally disparate cultures. It can be done, and Citigroup and JP Morgan Chase are dealing with some success with the problems involved, but for most of the firms named in these putative marriages the union would in our view be explosive!

As in commercial banking, the value of 'serial acquirers' has been clearly demonstrated. Firms like UBS and Citigroup have shown that lessons learned can be applied successfully to new acquisitions. In contrast, the market will understandably discount the ability of an acquisitions neophyte to succeed in this people-sensitive business.

In this context, how serious is the challenge of the big balance sheet of some of the newcomers to the incumbent Big Three US investment banks? Could this challenge be a key factor in driving such a merger?

In the fast-moving world of investment banking, one is inclined never to say 'never', but in our view this driver is unlikely to be a deciding factor. The dominant position of the Big Three in M & A and equities has been sustained for decades despite perennial efforts to dislodge them. The research by Greenwich Associates on the duration of the average lead investment banking relationship (see Table 3.1) supports the efforts made by firms like Goldman Sachs to build them over a period of decades. As Lisa Endlich in her book on Goldman explains:

> "There was a religion of client service ... The true value of the franchise lay in the length and depth of many of the firm's corporate relationships ... they had been nurtured by generations of bankers and handed down almost like family heirlooms. Devotion to the firm's clients was considered inviolate and formed the bedrock on which the firm's investment banking division sat."[41]

Times, people and circumstances change, but this service mentality is extraordinarily difficult to recreate. Firms like Goldman may 'lose the magic', to use the phrase of one of our Scandinavian friends, but in our view it is their game to lose.

What strikes us in particular in the primacy of the leading US investment banks in the advisory and equity issuance businesses is their parallel dominance of the desired operating model. It is one thing to dominate with a perennially successful business model, but that leadership becomes even more secure when the rivals are attempting to conquer with the same operational practices and processes.

One can foresee a few of the challengers finally replicating the Goldman/ Morgan Stanley 'one-firm' culture with all of its unique attributes, but at a minimum the effort will have to be sustained over a period of years to come.

The final negative for a commercial/investment bank merger is the commodity nature of the core loan product for commercial banks. How attractive would it be for an investment bank to take on the risks of such a merger simply to be able to lend more money at a single-digit return on attributable funds? We tend to agree with Marcel Ospel:

> *"It's not a big issue. Lending will suffer more from cycles than advisory-led products. We'll see a few banks stupidly buy market share, but as a business it can't be justified by the risk/reward equation."*

In sum, such mergers may well take place, but we believe other factors than simple access to a larger balance sheet will play a major role. Goldman Sachs and Morgan Stanley may lose a few relationships and allocate some additional resources to preserve others, but the basic model should survive the credit-led assault.

Another key issue apart from consolidation itself is the industry's likely future segmentation. In the previous chapter we recorded the majority view on the future dominance of today's global bulge group at the cost of mid-sized players and specialist firms.

In shaping our own view, we have been struck by the almost identical strategies followed by the eight global leaders. Figure 12.3 derived from a recent Sanford Bernstein report neatly summarizes both the focus of these firms on M & A and equities as well as the specific techniques being used to implement the strategy.

The issue is not just the simple one of 'eight into three (top market share slots) won't go'. It is also the lack of differentiation in the strategy and tactics of those eight firms, each of which seems to the outsider to be employing the same play book. In other businesses, this is not a recipe for success in confronting a well-positioned incumbent.

Unless the economics of operational leverage in these businesses is totally different from the impression given by our interview sample, this differentiation will take place in the months and years to come. Some competitors may abandon the M & A and equities effort entirely, faced with a continued revenue drought and a high cost base. Others may specialize in priority sectors and geographies. And still others will make every effort either to convince one of the leaders to join forces in a merger or to buy up a specialist advisory firm.

Figure 12.3 Virtually identical business models for global leaders

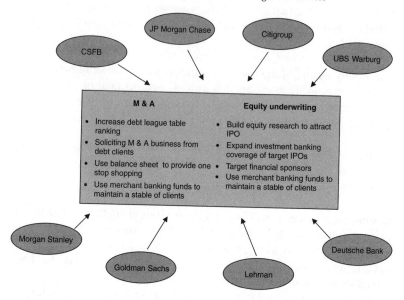

Source: Sanford Bernstein.

In sum, the power of established franchises in the desirable segments is awesome. As Figure 12.4 shows, in the three major segments the top five competitors have garnered at least 45 per cent of the fee pool, with similar market shares in the secondary markets. While the top five vary from year to year, we have seen in Table 2.1 that few new names have been added to the leadership during the past decade.

We thus share the view of observers such as Oliver, Wyman & Co. who foresee increased differentiation rather than convergence. There are worse fates, for example, than reconciling oneself to a role as a European-focused, rather than totally global, M & A and equities player, or a focused global fixed income and derivatives specialist. Clearly such a major decision will also be driven by the duration and depth of the revenue drought; a bank's cost base, product profitability and client profile; and the personal agenda of its leadership, but greater differentiation there will probably be.

This increased differentiation and diversity may well spread throughout the sector as the mid-sized European and other banks shape their strategies in a difficult operating environment. We are inclined to agree with Robert Statius-Muller and others who envisage the possibility of geography playing a greater role than in the past few years. And our interviews with banks such as BNP Paribas, Société Générale and SHB confirm that the message has been received and action taken.

The challenge for the mid-sized European banks – those below the three acknowledged European globals – is indeed a formidable one. They confront two separate mountains to climb: finding a profitable business model, and, arguably even more difficult, achieving the 'one-bank' operational model.

The key to the business model enigma lies in the popular phase 'scalability'. In Chapter 3 we recited some of the attributes of this model: focus on home country/local relationships, specializing in research on home country firms, tailoring the product range to that core client base, building local placing power, and so on. But can it all be done and still earn an acceptable return on capital employed? Is the 'home' market big and active enough? Is the necessary cost base too expensive? Is there another local competitor better positioned? We are in no position to answer these questions, but they must be provoking considerable debate in a number of mid-sized banks.

As for the operational model whose icon is Goldman Sachs, one can be a bit more specific. The contrast between the commercial and investment banking models depicted in Table 4.1 has not basically changed since *Doing Deals* was written some 15 years ago. The human turmoil

Figure 12.4 Leading players have disproportionately large market share

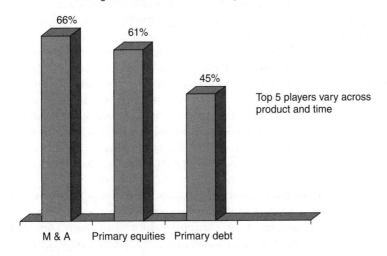

2001 global market share for five top firms

Top 5 players vary across product and time

Source: Crédit Suisse First Boston.

and travail in the 1990s of converting essentially commercial banks such as Deutsche Bank, the two Swiss banks and the original JP Morgan into fully-fledged investment banks is not likely to be embraced by many other candidates, especially those with alternative uses of capital such as retail banking and fund management.

A true fusion of commercial and investment banking functions, a Goldman-type customer coverage model, the introduction of a single bonus pool across these businesses, and the undertaking of a higher level of market risk – all these challenges are likely to constitute a bridge too far for most of these banks. And while this necessarily long-term effort is under way, greater financial transparency will drive investors, as they did in the case of the UK clearing banks in the early 1990s, to query the value of the whole exercise.

Yet a number of such European banks are well embarked on the voyage for both the business and operational destinations. The French market is probably large enough for several such successful competitors, while structural change may come to the German market in time to sustain the hopes of its aspirants. The market sizing given in Table 3.4 could be a starting point for this analysis.

On balance, however, we believe that only a small number of European banks will succeed in developing both a profitable business strategy and an operational model to sustain it. For the others, the combination of resistance from a commercial banking-dominated management and culture, stockholder influence in favour of re-allocating resources to other businesses, and sustained pressure from global and local investment banking competitors will eventually marginalize the investment banking function.

One possible solution has been suggested to resolve their dilemma: a cross-border merger of two leading European banks to create critical mass in investment banking. Putting aside the generic issue of whether such mergers add stockholder value, we would seriously question whether they could succeed in investment banking. While the potential market would increase in size, our guess is that such gains would be severely eroded by internal conflict and resistance to change. The result might well be two sub-scale businesses rather than one. The recent failed merger of two such second-tier investment banking businesses, Rabobank and DG Bank, is one indication of these pitfalls.

Diversity could also be generated by more banks reshaping their businesses around a limited number of sectors where they have a clear competitive advantage. One consulting firm thus advocates such 'multi-specialist' strategies. As friends like Lars Bertmar point out, any specialization or 'niche' implies risk – the risk of adverse market movements, competitors invading that niche, and the lack of inherent diversification enjoyed by the global firms.

As many of our friends tell us, success in investment banking is very much a function of taking bets. For Goldman in the early 1990s, it was a bet on global expansion. Later, for the Big Three US investment banks, it was a highly remunerative bet on the TMT sector. Will structural change in Europe – specifically Germany – now be such a successful bet, or will it become, like Merrill Lynch in the Japanese retail sector, yet another bet on convergence that takes too long to pay out for the stockholders? Eager exporters of American technology have blunted their lance before on resistance to change in Europe, and the restructuring of German industry and finance could well exceed the time frame imposed by impatient investors.

But the alternative is probably another form of risk – that of being marginalized by the global firms, as has been the case in the European market in recent years. And the sustained success of specialist firms like Fox-Pitt Kelton, Macquarie, Carnegie and Cazenove shows that the model is a viable one.

In sum, investment banking is truly the ultimate networking business. Key relationships of trust and communication exist within the successful investment bank and between these networks and the client. As so many of our interviewees have confirmed, success is largely a function of pooling information and relationships among trusted colleagues and clients. Individual banking entities come and go, but most of the professionals remain in the business to sustain their relationships with former colleagues and clients.

While these networks are the key to success, investment banks are also riddled with natural conflicts. Quite apart from the generic issues pitting the product, client and geographical elements of a global institution against each other, investment banks have their own special conflicts to address. Traders and bankers battling over bonuses and capital allocation, the use of customer information for frontrunning and proprietary trading, maintaining the independence of research, fund managers or private bankers reluctant to act as 'stuffees' for their clients – all demand a unique blend of leadership and cultural values for resolution.

The most successful firms to date, whether a global entity like Morgan Stanley or a regional specialist like Carnegie, have grown organically over a period of decades through the development of these networks. There is no reason why they cannot be replicated through the merger route, but that will inevitably require strong leadership, plenty of time and the development of common values. In the meantime new entities will spin off from the larger ones as individual practitioners seek to recreate the 'old' culture and values.

We frankly doubt, however, whether very many rivals to Goldman Sachs and Morgan Stanley will succeed in this effort in the next three to five years. Global players formed from acquisitions or the cobbling together of teams recruited from the market are miles away from any true 'one-firm' culture. Even Citigroup, as Hans Morris has acknowledged, has a long way to go even after three to four years of integrating its commercial and investment banking arms – despite extraordinary leadership and a unique array of strengths.

And for most mid-sized European banks, as mentioned above, the dual challenge of finding a viable business model and replicating the Goldman Sachs operating model will probably defeat even the best of intentions.

One of the most fascinating revelations of our research is the extent of consensus in the business on best practice – specifically the operating model associated with Goldman Sachs. Designed to ensure the banker's mantra of successful execution, this 'one-firm' culture is the strategic objective of a multiplicity of competitors. We have seen how, for example, it plays an integral role in minimizing operational risk. And for firms reshaping their business to adapt to today's changed market conditions, a 'one-firm' culture would seem essential to convincing specialist bankers to move to a totally different role in the firm. One can only imagine a veteran TMT specialist being told that his future lies in conversion to a public utility career!

Thus the long-term outlook for investment is a fascinating amalgam of continuity and change: the continuity of networks, and the change imposed by market conditions and opportunities, client needs and the creativity of individual bankers. Positioning in the league tables in relationship-driven businesses like M & A bears witness to the strength of continuity.

As for change, it is built into a business shaped around managing a multitude of risks and the inherent volatility of markets. Investment bankers are adept at discovering new ways to make – and lose – money. Our analysis of risks in Chapter 7 confirms that 'hundred year floods' will continue to occur every few years, whatever VAR or other models are used, as banks push the envelope to maximize revenues. These disasters, in particular those created by fraud, will occasionally sweep away firms in the future as they have in the past. And the current revenue drought will probably play its role in reshaping the business after a decade of unprecedented expansion.

Notes

Full details for all publications are given in the Bibliography.

1. See bibliography for Auletta (*Greed and Glory on Wall Street*), Hobson (*The Pride of Lucifer*), and Vander Weyer (*Falling Eagle*).
2. See bibliography for Augar (*The Death of Gentlemanly Capitalism*), Endlich (*Goldman Sachs: the Culture of Success*), and Lewis (*Liar's Poker*).
3. Crane *et al.*, *Doing Deals*.
4. Gaulard, *European Investment Banking: Beyond Volatility*.
5. Greenwich Associates, *Financial Services Without Borders*, p. 221.
6. Ibid., pp. 222–6.
7. Augar, *The Death of Gentlemanly Capitalism*, p. 136.
8. Ibid., p. 166.
9. Hobson, *The Pride of Lucifer*, p. 267.
10. Davis, *Leadership in Financial Services*, pp. 122–3.
11. *Financial Times*, 13 April 2002, p. 5.
12. Crane *et al.*, *Doing Deals*, pp. 121–2.
13. Ibid., p. 33.
14. Greenwich Associates, *Financial Services Without Borders*, p. 157.
15. Ibid., p. 78.
16. Gresch *et al.*, *Investment Banking Puzzles*, pp. 11–12.
17. Crédit Suisse First Boston, Presentation.
18. Greenwich Associates, *Financial Services Without Borders*, pp. 49–65.
19. Ibid., p. 157.
20. Crane *et al.*, Doing Deals, pp. 38–46.
21. Lewis, *Liar's Poker*, p. 81.
22. Augar, *The Death of Gentlemanly Capitalism*, p. 262.
23. Davis, *Leadership in Financial Services*, p. 124.
24. Crane *et al.*, *Doing Deals*, p. 3.
25. Ibid., p. 66.
26. Lewis, *Liar's Poker*, pp. 105, 237.
27. Crane *et al.*, *Doing Deals*, p. 165.
28. *Financial Times*, 21 May 2002.
29. Endlich, *Goldman Sachs*, p. 19
30. Shawn Tully, *Fortune*, 15 April 2002.
31. Endlich, *Goldman Sachs*, p. 199.
32. McKinsey & Co./JP Morgan, *The Future of Equity Trading in Europe*.
33. Kathryn Tully, *Euromoney*, pp. 70–5.
34. Ibid.
35. Davis, *Bank Mergers*.
36. Ibid., p. 70.

37. Ibid., p. 78.
38. Cairns, *The Limits of Bank Convergence.*
39. Oliver, Wyman & Co./Morgan Stanley.
40. Moszkowski, *Capital Punishment.*
41. Endlich, *Goldman Sachs.*
42. *Financial Times*, 8 January 2002, p. 9.

Appendix 1: List of Institutions Interviewed

Investment banks

ABN Amro
Barclays Capital
BNP Paribas
Carnegie Group
Cazenove & Co
Citigroup
Crédit Suisse First Boston
Deutsche Bank
Dresdner Kleinwort Wasserstein
Enskilda Securities
Fox-Pitt Kelton Inc
Goldman Sachs
Handelsbanken
Hawkpoint
HSBC
ING Barings
JP Morgan Chase
Lazard Brothers
Lehman Brothers
Macquarie Bank
Merrill Lynch
Morgan Stanley Dean Witter
N M Rothschild & Sons
Nomura International
Nordea
Société Générale
UBS Warburg

Industry specialists

Boston Consulting Group
First Consulting
Fitch
Freeman & Company
Goldman Sachs (research group)
Greenwich Associates
Harvard Business School
JP Morgan Chase (research group)
McKinsey & Company
Oliver, Wyman & Company
Risk Management Association
Sanford Bernstein
Martin Smith
Soifer Consulting
Stern School of Business

Appendix 2: The 14 Core Values of Goldman Sachs

1. Our clients' interest always come first. Our experience shows that if we serve our clients well, our own success will follow.
2. Our assets are our people, capital and reputation. If any of these is ever diminished, the last is the most difficult to restore. We are dedicated to complying fully with the letter and spirit of the laws, rules and ethical principles that govern us. Our continued success depends upon unswerving adherence to this standard.
3. Our goal is to provide superior returns to our shareholders. Profitability is critical to achieving superior returns, building our capital, and attracting and keeping our best people. Significant employee stock ownership aligns the interest of our employees and our shareholders.
4. We take great pride in the professional quality of our work. We have an uncompromising determination to achieve excellence in everything we undertake. Though we may be involved in a wide variety and heavy volume of activity, we would, if it came to a choice, rather be best than biggest.
5. We stress creativity and imagination in everything we do. While recognizing that the old may still be the best way, we constantly strive to find a better solution to a client's problem. We pride ourselves on having pioneered many of the practices and techniques that have become standard in the industry.
6. We make an unusual effort to identify and recruit the very best person for every job. Although our activities are measured in billions of dollars, we select our people one by one. In a service business, we know that without the best people, we cannot be the best firm.
7. We offer our people the opportunity to move ahead more rapidly than is possible at most other places. Advancement depends on merit and we have yet to find the limits to the responsibility our best people are able to assume. For us to be successful, our men and women must reflect the diversity of the communities and cultures in which we operate. That means we must attract, retain and motivate people from many backgrounds and perspectives. Being diverse is not optional; it is what we must be.
8. We stress teamwork in everything we do. While individual creativity is always encouraged, we have found that team effort often produces the best results. We have no room for those who put their personal interests ahead of the interests of the firm and its clients.
9. The dedication of our people to the firm and the intense effort they give their jobs are greater than one finds in most other organizations. We think that this is an important part of our success.
10. We consider our size an asset that we try hard to preserve. We want to be big enough to undertake the largest project that any of our clients could contemplate, yet small enough to maintain the loyalty, the intimacy and the esprit de corps that we all treasure and that contribute greatly to our success.

11. We constantly strive to anticipate the rapidly changing needs of our clients and to develop new services to meet those needs. We know that the world of finance will not stand still and that complacency can lead to extinction.
12. We regularly receive confidential information as part of our normal client relationships. To breach a confidence or to use confidential information improperly or carelessly would be unthinkable.
13. Our business is highly competitive, and we aggressively seek to expand our client relationships. However, we must always be fair competitors and must never denigrate other firms.
14. Integrity and honesty are at the heart of our business. We expect our people to maintain high ethical standards in everything they do, both in their work for the firm and in their personal lives.

Source: 2001 Annual Report.

Bibliography

Augar, Philip, *The Death of Gentlemanly Capitalism*, London, Penguin Books, 2000.

Auletta, Ken, *Greed and Glory on Wall Street: The Fall of the House of Lehman*, New York, Random House, 1986.

Cairns, Alastair J. *et al.*, 'The limits of bank convergence', *McKinsey Quarterly*, number 2, New York, 2002.

Crane, Dwight, Robert Eccles *et al.*, *Doing Deals: Investment Banks at Work*, Boston, MA, Harvard Business School Press, 1988.

Crédit Suisse First Boston, Presentation to UBS Warburg Conference, April 2002, New York.

Davis, Steven I. *Bank Mergers*, London, Macmillan, 2000.

Davis, Steven I. *Leadership In Financial Services*, London, Macmillan, 1997.

Economist Intelligence Unit, *Global Investment Banking: Insights from industry leaders*, written in collaboration with AT Kearney, Inc., London, 1998.

Endlich, Lisa, *Goldman Sachs: the Culture of Success*, New York, Alfred A Knopf, Inc., 1999.

Financial Times, 13 April 2002, pp. 9–15 (Charles Pretzlik article on Goldman Sachs).

Financial Times, 21 May 2002.

Gaulard, Jacques-Henri *et al.*, *European Investment Banking: Beyond Volatility*, London, Lehman Brothers, 2001.

Goldman Sachs and McKinsey & Company, *The Future of Corporate Banking in Europe*, London, 2001.

Greenwich Associates, Financial Services without Borders: How to succeed in professional financial services, New York, John Wiley & Sons, 2001.

Gresch, Daniel *et al.*, *Investment Banking Puzzles: Diving into the Fee Pool*, UBS Warburg, Zurich, 20 May 2002.

Hintz, Brad, *Brokerage Industry: Trees Don't Grow to the Sky*, Bernstein Research, New York, 20 May 2002.

Hobson, Dominic, *The Pride of Lucifer: the Unauthorised Biography of a Merchant Bank*, London, Hamish Hamilton, 1990.

Leonard, John *et al.*, *Global Investment Banking: Which New Players will Make the Team?*, New York, Salomon Brothers, February 1994.

Lewis, Michael, *Liar's Poker*, London, Hodder & Stoughton, 1989.

McKinsey & Co and JP Morgan Securities Ltd, *The Future of Equity Trading in Europe: Balancing Scale, Scope and Segmentation*, London, 20 May 2002.

Moszkowski, Guy *et al.*, *Capital Punishment? Investment Banks Confront Loan Demand*, Salomon Smith Barney, New York, 2001.

Nerby, Peter *et al.*, *US Securities Firms: Tightening the Belt – Industry Outlook 2002*, Moody's Investors Service, New York, January 2002

Oliver Wyman & Co. and Morgan Stanley, *The Future of European Corporate and Investment Banking: The Need to Differentiate*, London, 2002.

Ramsden, Richard *et al.*, *Investment Banking Update: Europe*, Goldman Sachs, London, 2002.

Smith, Roy C. and Walter, Ingo, *Global Wholesale Finance: Structure, Conduct, Performance*, paper submitted by Stern School of Business to 22nd SUERF Colloquium, Vienna, 2000.

Tully, Kathryn, 'The big spenders learn to budget', *Euromoney*, March 2002, pp. 70–75, London, 20 May 2002.

Tully, Shawn, 'Risky Business', *Fortune*, 15 April 2002, New York, 2002.

Vander Weyer, Martin, *Falling Eagle: the Decline of Barclays Bank*, London, Weidenfeld & Nicolson, 2000.

Index